£2·95

THE FIREPLACE IN THE HOME

The Fireplace in the Home

TRUDY WEST

Line Illustrations by P. C. Young

DAVID & CHARLES
NEWTON ABBOT   LONDON
NORTH POMFRET (VT)   VANCOUVER

ISBN 0 7153 6751 X
Library of Congress Catalog Card Number 74-81060
© Trudy West 1976

Set in 11 on 13pt Plantin and printed in
Great Britain by Redwood Burn Limited, Trowbridge & Esher
for David & Charles (Publishers) Limited
Brunel House   Newton Abbot   Devon

Published in the United States of America
by David & Charles Inc   North Pomfret
Vermont 05053   USA

Published in Canada
by Douglas David & Charles Limited
1875 Welch Street   North Vancouver BC

Contents

Acknowledgements

I am grateful for leave to quote from *Building in England Down to 1540* by L. F. Salzman, by permission of the publishers, The Clarendon Press, Oxford; *The House and Home* by M. W. Barley, (1963), by permission of Studio Vista; *The English Fireplace* by L. A. Shuffrey, by permission of B. T. Batsford Ltd.

I also thank the many professional bodies, commercial organisations and others who granted research facilities, particularly the following:

The Weald & Downland Open Air Museum, the Avoncroft Museum of Buildings, the Victoria & Albert Museum, Soane's Museum, the Oxford University Press, the Governors of Sutton's Hospital, Hatchard's Ltd, The Carron Company, Wm Barraclough Ltd, The Baxi Patent Fire Company, Esse Heaters, G. Jackson & Sons Ltd, H. & E. Smith Ltd, International Nickel Ltd, Kingsley Patent Fire Company, Repton Foundry (Scotland) Ltd, James Smellie Ltd, Smith & Wellstood (Mfg) Ltd, Grahamston Iron Company, Fulham Pottery.

Mr John Bell of A. Bell & Co Ltd, Mr L. A. Walters of Galleon Fireplaces Ltd, Mr D. J. Malkin of H. & R. Johnson, Mr P. W. Stevenson of the National Coal Board and many others assisted me.

For permission to quote examples from their homes and obtain photographs, I am greatly indebted to Viscount de L'Isle, VC, KG, the Marquess of Exeter, the Earl of Pembroke, the Duke of Bedford, the Duke of Atholl, the Hon David Lytton-Cobbold, Major More-Molyneux, Mr George Howard, Mr and Mrs Derek Simmons, Mr and Mrs Anthony Vaughan, Mr Roger Board.

Illustrations

Preface

'No place is more delightful than one's own fireside.' Cicero's words spoken over 2,000 years ago, still have a ring of truth in them, though man's conception of his fireside has changed greatly over the centuries. Whatever its form, it has always been regarded with affection – even sentiment at times, as signifying the heart of the British home, the place where the family foregathers, a focal point of warmth and comfort, a necessity in this cold and changeable climate.

Admittedly, it has a great deal of competition today, when central heating has become standard; but there has recently been a great revival of interest in the fireplace and its design. The friendly glow of a living, open fire is again taking its rightful place at the centre of the home and history has come full circle. Modern science ensures that it is also efficient and economical and it has been proved conclusively that it is the most healthy way of heating a room and by far the kindest to good furniture.

In tracing the history of the fireplace, I have as far as possible, without limiting the text, used as examples fireplaces which may be seen by the public. I hope this will enhance enjoyment of that unique institution, the open fireplace, and appreciation of the design and ornament of outstanding examples.

T.W.

1 Tudor fireplace in a fifteenth-century cottage at Lindfield, Sussex. The firebasket and canopy are fairly modern additions

1

The Central Hearth

Fire is at once man's greatest enemy and his greatest friend. It has an elemental force and majesty that appeals to the primitive in man. It is at the heart of some of the most fascinating folklore and legends in the world. It weaves itself into the dreams and magic of a child's imagination as he watches the changing shapes in its flames.

It is something, indeed, from which we have built up our civilization, for there has been a place for a fire in the home from the dawn of time, whether it be in cave or castle. So the history of the fireplace is not only an architectural story; it is the history of a people in the intimacy of their homes, the story of a way of life dictated by the fundamental basic need for warmth and security, and later by changing fashions and social attitudes.

Man has always readily adapted himself to his environment and we may assume that primitive man made a fire where and when he had need of one. He came to terms with fire and learned how to create flames at will by means of flint sparks. The discovery of controllable heat set him free to travel in other zones, because it gave him warmth, the means of cooking and illumination: it gave him the domestic hearth in the family cave and this in turn helped to establish friendly family relationships.

In the New Stone Age he also made a fire in a hole outside his hut. After the fire had burnt out he put food to cook in the hole, heaping

2 Fourteenth-century central hearth at Penshurst Place, Kent, with coupled andirons

turves over it to retain the heat. It was a primitive but efficient method of cooking which persisted for centuries in many country districts.

It was not until the Roman occupation of Britain that we hear of any specialised form of heating for the home. The Romans developed an ingenious system of central heating, designed primarily to mitigate the rigours of the English climate for these Mediterranean invaders. Their hypocausts, or heating chambers under the floor, seem to have worked very well; and they used movable braziers in which they burned charcoal.

There is also some archaeological evidence of open fireplaces having been used. In the Roman villa at Bignor, Sussex, open fireplaces and hearths of tiles were found in two of the rooms and it was deduced from the available evidence that such a fireplace, against a wall, probably had a hood over it to conduct smoke by a pipe laid up the wall to a vent in the roof.

In many ways, it was a civilization ahead of its time, and the semi-barbarian Saxon invaders who came after destroyed it ruthlessly. Probably the Roman method of heating would have been unsuitable for the wooden buildings of the Saxons, for they were essentially farmers and they preferred their traditional ways, living in villages of their own making.

They evolved a distinctive type of dwelling, consisting of a common hall, or house place, often some 30 to 40ft in length and about half that in width. It provided shelter from the elements and for the next two centuries at least it often formed the sole living-room, sleeping-room and kitchen for the owner and his family, his guests and his serfs. A huge log fire on a central hearth provided warmth, the smoke escaping through an opening in the roof.

The well-to-do farmer divided these barn-like halls into bays which he at first shared with his cattle; later, when the beasts were turned out into byres, it became a great hall with room for house servants and a permanent fire hearth at the upper end. The triangular space at each end of the building formed by the apices of the rafters and their connecting collars was left open to allow the smoke to escape.

All these homes, humble or great, shared a common feature: the central hearth, where a fire of wood, peat, turf or charcoal was made, sometimes on the beaten-earth floor, sometimes on a great stone slab set in the middle of the room.

In the primitive hut of the peasant the centre of the earth floor would be excavated to a depth of about 18 inches and the hearth stone set into the hollow thus formed, the occupants sleeping on the platforms around it and forming, quite literally, the 'family circle'.

The smoke had to escape where it might, through the thatch or through a 'wind-hole' cut in the wall. There is no doubt that the room was sooty, particularly where the space was confined. Chaucer describes a widow's 'sooty bower' in *The Tale of a Nun's Priest*; the situation had to be accepted if one desired to keep warm.

It is difficult, on the slender archaeological evidence available, to build up an accurate picture of the domestic life of this period and we may be doing the Saxons an injustice by assuming that it was without any kind of comfort; for the central fire, burning by night as well as day, supplying heat and a means of cooking, was shared by all in a kind of cosy intimacy that fostered family life and gave a sense of security from marauding wild beasts.

After the Norman Conquest, the great castles the Normans built for themselves are not exactly our idea of comfort. The thick stone walls had openings for windows, perhaps protected by oak shutters, the stone floors were covered only with rushes, and the central hearth in the common hall was the only means of heating, apart from braziers. This was 'home' for the nobility.

The Normans also built great moated manors for defensive purposes, and the nucleus of the building was invariably the Great Hall. Part of the reason for its lofty height, open to the rafters, was the necessity for making an adequate place for a fire, and the hearth was permanently placed near the dais end. The servants ate and slept round it, while their lord occupied the raised dais with his family and guests, so that all shared the warmth and an intimate communal life as they 'gathered round the fire'. The cooking fire was then relegated to a separate kitchen, connected to the hall by a covered way.

When the lord and his family began to desire more privacy, they

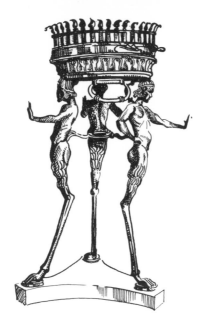

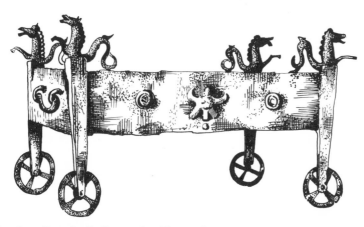

3 Brazier after the Italian style. Charcoal, which was prepared outside the
room and brought in when burning well in the movable fire below, was put
into the top section

built flanking wings at each end of the hall, comprising a service wing and a solar. The service wing would have its own cooking fire whilst the solar would in all probability be heated by a brazier. Thus for the first time the feudal lord dispensed with his old intimate connections with his 'hearth men', who no longer sat at the same fire or shared the same dormitory with him.

Heating by means of a brazier, the system generally used by the Greeks and Romans, was still used in warm countries until quite a late date. Braziers formed attractive pieces of furniture, often beautifully ornamented. Their advantage was that all the heat they generated went to warm the room, their great disadvantage the fact that in most cases there was no provision made for the outlet of smoke. In a small enclosed room the heat and smoke must soon have become so overpowering that the occupants must have been forced to open a window or shutter.

An iron brazier filled with charcoal sometimes stood on the central hearth instead of a fire of wood, but in Norman England the brazier seems to have been more of a passing convenience, to warm the smaller chambers; the central hearth with its log fire continued to take pride of place in the home.

In a great house it would be made up of more than one huge slab of stone, with great billet bars to support the roaring logs, the flames and smoke leaping upwards to escape through a vent, or louvre, in the form of a turret set in the high open roof over the hearth; the timbers were blackened and many a priceless wall hanging or tapestry ruined as they did so.

There was also the ever-present risk of fire, particularly where the floor was strewn with rushes and straw and where timbers were exposed. It was probably because of this danger that the curfew was first introduced. The word originates from the French *couvre feu*, cover fire, and the tolling of the church bell at 8 o'clock, or some other hour in the evening, was the signal for people to cover their fires and retire for the night. The practice has been attributed by some to William the Conqueror who, in 1068, is said to have introduced it as a means of preventing the English from assembling round their fires in the evening in order to concoct plans of rebellion.

The curfew also gave its name to a cover for putting over the fire. Made of quite thin metal so that the embers would still be burning in the morning, some of these covers became ornamental objects in themselves.

There are very few original central hearths left intact today; they were phased out of existence many generations ago. There is, however, a very fine fourteenth-century central fireplace at Penshurst Place, Kent, one of England's most historic stately homes, belonging to the Sidney family from the time of Edward III. The fireplace is in the Baron's Hall – the finest domestic hall of the fourteenth century left to us – and it has a massive double trestle of wrought iron to take the burning logs, each stanchion embossed with the Sidney coat of arms, consisting of a double pheon or broad arrow. Firedogs coupled in this manner are known to be of great antiquity. The hearth itself is a brick-paved octagonal space, 8ft across, level with the floor and surrounded by a low curb (shown earlier in this chapter). The smoke drifted up to the great vaulted chestnut roof (probably the only one of its kind in existence) and thence through a vent, long since closed. (The present owner of Penshurst Place, Lord de L'Isle, allows public access to the state rooms.)

There are also relics of the central hearth in the Great Hall at Hampton Court Palace, but this only shows the actual stone let into the floor at the dais end. It was on this dais, raised one step above the floor of the main hall that the high table was set for the king and his guests, while the rest of the company sat at tables ranging down each side of the hall. From the size of the stone, those seated nearest the fire must have been uncomfortably hot; they may have been the users of the fire screens, standing on feet, which were in use in the thirteenth century.

On a smaller scale, there is still evidence of the central hearth in houses and cottages of the early medieval period. One such is at the fourteenth-century priest's house at Alfriston, Sussex, where traces remain on the beaten-earth floor in the open hall. This house is preserved by the National Trust and can be visited.

It is relatively easy to trace where a central fireplace would have been by the smoke-blackened, soot-encrusted timbers in the roof, and such evidence may be found in many old houses of up to the sixteenth century, for the central hearth survived until that period in most houses in Kent and Essex, and to a lesser degree in other counties as well.

In its favour it must be said that it was cheap and simple and radiated the heat so that none was lost. Nor was it a bad ventilator, since no impure air could remain in the room and any cold draughts entering would not be drawn to a single spot. It would therefore be less concentrated and less injurious to health than foul air. On the other hand, the smoke was undoubtedly a great nuisance and certainly ruined many fine pictures and wall hangings.

We have to rely mainly on museums for an authentic picture of the early medieval domestic hearth, and some of the open-air museums are doing invaluable work in this respect. In the Weald & Downland Open Air Museum at Singleton, Sussex, there are reconstructions of buildings from medieval times to the early nineteenth century. One of the most interesting exhibits is that of a mid-thirteenth century cottage which was excavated at Hangleton, a village which was completely abandoned, possibly after the Black Death. Archaeological findings show a large oven in one corner of a room farthest from the entrance, and it is likely that the owner was a baker. This was the kitchen portion, partitioned off from the open hall. Unfortunately, only fragments of the hearth remained, but it was sufficient to show that it was constructed of tiles set on edge – a common medieval form. It was a fairly lofty hall for such a small cottage, the gables being 13ft above the floor level, so the smoke would normally accumulate above the level of the collars of the roof timbers, and, we assume, find its way out through the gables.

Winkhurst House, another reconstruction at Singleton, again shows the central hearth in the open hall, and here a cauldron is suspended on a chain from a great beam above the fire, representing the simple method of cooking common to the times. Sooting on the original roof timbers proved the position of the triangular smoke-vent in the west gable and this was apparently the sole means of drawing smoke and cooking smells away from the hall.

The Avoncroft Museum of Buildings at Stoke Prior, Worcestershire, has a fifteenth-century merchant's house with the central hearth reconstructed in its original form. It is interesting to compare examples where and when they can be found, and it is thanks to the various museums of buildings that we can get an accurate idea of the central fireplace in the average early medieval home.

It was not until about the end of the twelfth century that the smoke hole in the roof was given a raised canopy with louvred sides, a louvre, from the French *l'ouvert*, opening. The aperture was generally octagonal but sometimes square in shape. From this rose the turret with openings to the outer air so formed as to exclude the rain and let the smoke out. (Louvre boards are used in a similar way today.)

The Great Halls, such as those at Penshurst Place and Hampton Court Palace which preserve the central hearth so carefully, have dispensed with all signs of the original smoke-vents, but from old accounts they must have been of great magnificence, elaborately decorated, painted and gilded. Fortunately numerous louvres remain in buildings of the fifteenth and sixteenth centuries, particularly in some old colleges. Two which are well preserved and easily seen are on

4 Existing sixteenth-century smoke louvres on (a) Staple Inn, Holborn and (b) Barnard's Inn, Holborn

Barnard's Inn, Holborn, and Staple Inn, Holborn. Both date from the sixteenth century.

There are still survivals of the louvred turret on some old manor houses, but they usually house a clock or a bell and their original purpose is obscured. Some were filled with glass to act as a lantern, as at Trinity College, Cambridge, but many more must have fallen into disuse, and so decayed and been pulled down. The practical necessity of carrying away smoke provided the reason for what could be very picturesque architectural features, which effectively broke the long line of a hall roof – at least the more decorative ones did, but according to ancient records there were some very makeshift appliances set up on the roofs of humbler homes.

Chaucer's 'poor widow' again reminds us of the plight of humble folk.

> Of one bay's breadth, God wot! a silly cote,
> Whose thatchèd sparres are furr'd with sluttish soote
> A whole inch thick, shining, like black-moor's brows,
> Through smok that down the head-les barrel blows.

L. F. Salzman in his book *Building in England Down to 1540* describes a simple method of using a barrel with the ends knocked out – the 'head-les barrel', in fact, and quotes from an old invoice, '4d. paid for a cask for a louver at Cambridge in 1415'.

2

The Wall Fireplace

The most significant development in the history of the fireplace came about mainly through the building of great strongholds and abbeys which, with their multiple storeys, made the central hearth virtually useless.

The Normans built their fortresses for defence purposes and the roof was a battlement, so that it became impossible to have a central opening for the escape of smoke. The Norman keep was, in fact, a strongly fortified house, considerably more comfortable than the primitive castles, if still rough and chilly to our eyes. These master builders quickly realised that the fireplace need not necessarily remain in the middle of a room, but could more conveniently be placed against a wall protected by a stone reredos or fireback. So they placed the hearth stone against the inner side of an outer wall, with a rudimentary flue rising obliquely within the thickness of the wall, ending in a vent hole or vertical aperture in the outer wall. Still only the most palatial keeps aspired to these fireplaces.

Very early examples are to be seen in the great strongholds erected immediately after the Conquest, such as those at Rochester, Colchester and Castle Hedingham, reputed to be the best-preserved stone Norman building in England. Some of these fireplaces are no more than shallow recesses within the thickness of the wall, lined with thin bricks or tiles laid in horizontal courses or in herringbone pattern.

Brick or tile in some form was used continuously after the Norman period, and some very fine work was created from the twelfth century onwards. It is easy to detect Roman bricks being reused by their large flat shape, and there are many of these to be seen in areas which were great Roman settlements.

The fireplace recess was shallow at the level of the floor, deepening as it rose upward and forming a wide throat to the flue which divided

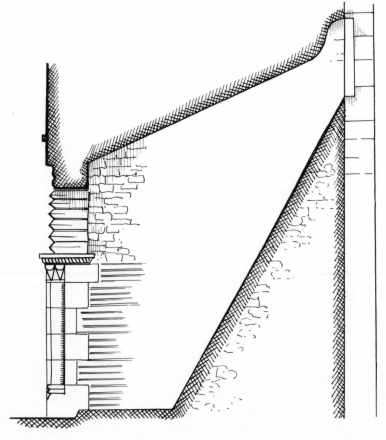

5 Section showing flue of fireplace in the state room at Castle Hedingham, Essex The flue discharged on either side of a flat buttress

6 Early English carved stone fireplace (now in the Victoria & Albert Museum)

as it neared the back wall to form vertical openings on the outside face. It seems that one external opening was not always enough to take the smoke away when the wind was in a certain direction, for at some of these old castles there are two – one at each side of a flat buttress. This arrangement at Castle Hedingham is shown on page 22.

Where the reredos was placed flat against the wall, a projecting stone hood, tapering upwards and backwards, covered the flue and collected the smoke, so the flue ending in a chimney, as we now know it, had its origins in the Norman period of architecture in England, gradually assuming a more functional design as the fireplace developed.

By the thirteenth century – the 'Early English' period – the fireplace had taken on a definite character and a progressive design. It was a time when people took great delight in carving in stone, and the Gothic stonemason lavished his considerable skill and artistry on carving the massive corbels which carried the hood. This was the earliest kind of art applied to the fireplace.

So we see the typical thirteenth-century fireplace as hooded, with engaged jamb shafts for support on each side of a shallow recess which sloped backwards and upwards. Some were slightly more recessed into the wall than others, but in general this kind of hooded stone fireplace continued to be built during the fourteenth century, with the mouldings and carvings changing in design according to the period.

Moulded jambs projecting from the wall in curves now formed the corbel to support the hood and the stonemason continued to exercise his skill in embellishing them.

A design of three-lobed leaves is characteristic of this Early English period, with bosses and foliage and heads in the centre – nearly always representing people of the day.

The painter as well as the sculptor used the fireplace as a showpiece for his art. Records tell us that at the time of Henry III, the Keeper of the King's Works at Westminster was ordered to paint the chimney of the Queen's chamber, 'and on it to cause to be portrayed a figure of Winter, which, as well as by its sad countenance as by other miserable contortions of the body, may be observedly likened to winter itself.' Another time the King commanded the sheriffs of Wiltshire to 'rebuild the chimney in our Queen's hall [at Clarendon] with two marble columns on each side of the chimney, and sculpture the mantel of the chimney with the twelve months of the year.'

It should be remembered that in medieval times the term 'chimney' included the whole of the fireplace, the hearth, the mantel, flue, or any of its parts, and not just the chimney shaft as we now understand it.

Domestic buildings, as well as castles, right up to the fifteenth century, were almost all built for defence, and the saying that 'an Englishman's home is his castle' was literally true. The keep of Tattershall Castle in Lincolnshire, built in 1440, one of the finest survivals of a fortified brick dwelling, is now in the care of the National Trust. Through this, and similar rare examples, we are able to get some idea of the emerging domesticity of this time. Manor houses were mostly fortified and moated also, with few rooms apart from the Great Hall, but as England became a little more settled under the feudal lords and barons, the big houses gradually expanded. The lord no longer dined with his retainers in the hall, but withdrew with his family to his solar, or chamber, at the upper end of the hall, and it was here, in my lady's bower, that the first wall fireplaces were built.

The position against a side wall not only made it easier to channel the smoke through a sloping hood, but also gave more room to the occupants; it was not long before these fireplaces found their way into the smaller apartments of the manor house, while the main hall, open to the roof, retained the central hearth.

The idea of the hood (sometimes referred to as a 'cover' in old manuscripts) over the fire was soon copied in smaller homes, though humble people could not aspire to stone. In timber-frame hall houses they built smoke shafts of wattle and daub, though the smoke still had to pass out through the roof as it obviously could not pass up through a panelled wall. The hood, like an inverted funnel made of wattle, timber, plaster or clay, held up by ironwork, was fixed to the wall above the reredos and drew most of the smoke upwards. (In some crofters' cottages in the Shetlands it is still possible to see a fire in the centre of the house with a stone back against which cooking is done – a survival of the ancient reredos.) The hood and the chimney-breast below often projected into the room for 3 or 4ft, and the shaft went up through the chamber above, sloping up to the louvre. It must have taken considerable space in a room but it did make it warm.

In a cruck house, where the great tie-beam is placed about 6ft above ground level, the smoke hood was made to slope upward from the tie-beam to the roof at the gable end. The fireplace opening was big enough to take all the customary cooking utensils as well as an inglenook. In some of the cruck houses in the Yorkshire dales there would be a 'witch post' supporting the cross beam with some strange carvings on it, the origins of which are shrouded in mystery. In the Ryedale Folk Museum at Hutton-le-Hole, Yorkshire, is a particularly fine example of one of these witch posts; this is a district where belief in magic was widespread for centuries and the local folklore is full of stories of witches and their mysterious powers. It is said they were powerless to enter or wreak harm in a room guarded by a witch post.

Though the clay of the daub of these smoke hoods hardened in the heat until it was almost like stone, there was still a great risk of fire, more especially in big towns where the houses were built mainly of wood and the floors were strewn with rushes. Moreover houses were huddled so closely together that in the fourteenth century regulations in the City of London forbade the placing of any reredos where a fire was made for cooking near partition walls of laths or boards, or elsewhere where there was danger of fire. Chimneys in future were to be made of stone, tiles or brick, and not of plaster or wood 'under pain of being pulled down'.

The chief fuel used was wood, though coal appears to have been used to a limited extent – and prohibited from time to time as a nuisance because of its unpleasant smoke and fumes. In those early days it was used for industry rather than the domestic hearth.

As new fireplaces were built they became more deeply recessed into the wall and eventually the hood was dispensed with on the assumption that it was no longer necessary. Buildings erected at the end of the fourteenth century had their fireplaces entirely recessed, the arch flush with the face of the wall. Many of these can be seen in castles of this period. In the old Clergy House at Alfriston, Sussex, there are fourteenth-century fire-openings in the rooms at the western end of the building, built one above the other.

Gothic architecture in general underwent such gradual periods of transition that it is sometimes difficult to detect where one period ends and another begins. This is particularly so when the heavier styles of Norman architecture were slowly being abandoned in favour of the Early English with its lighter lines and its accent on ecclesiastical building. Great monastic establishments were built at this time and, austere though they were in many respects, they had wall fireplaces built into many of the principal rooms. Some are quite beautiful in their way and show a fine sense of craftsmanship.

There is one in the Victoria & Albert Museum, bought from a house in Prittlewell, Essex, in 1906, which is reckoned to be of monastic origin, late fifteenth or early sixteenth century. It is basically of carved stone, with the spandrels filled with flowers and foliage. Above is a brickwork panel enclosing a Gothic arch with three compartments, the central one painted with the sacred monogram and those at the sides with fleur-de-lys. The carved brick is thinly coated with plaster. The stonework of the fireplace appears to be in six massive pieces. The two sides are not exactly the same size and the spandrels have different flowers and foliage: the stone on the right-hand side of the fireplace goes back to a depth of about 4ft 8in, that on the left is set in another way and runs outwards. In the back of the recess is a 'squint' – an aperture cut through the wall – with a sliding shutter (page 23).

This is an interesting fireplace and from the available records, it is thought to have been part of the property of a Guild or Fraternity of Jesus which existed as early as 1468, and to have been altered to its present state soon after the Dissolution. The squint may therefore have been directed to an altar.

By the fifteenth century the wall fireplace had been introduced into the lofty Great Hall of castle and manor house, and its importance as a focal point grew as it became more lavishly adorned. It had not yet ousted the central hearth, which continued to be used for some time.

The new fireplaces were usually built in a side wall below the dais and near the bay window. Wide and deep, they were generally lined with herringbone brickwork. The hearth was often raised a few inches from the floor and on it stood the great andirons, or firedogs, to support the weight of the huge logs and allow the air to circulate between them and keep them ablaze. All these hearths were made to take great roaring fires, sending currents of air sweeping through the building. The draughts must have been intolerable, particularly where the hall had doors on opposite walls. The builders tried to solve this problem, first by building a short wooden 'spur' screen inside the main door, with a similar one to the opposite door. Later, a further improvement was made by filling in the gap between the ends of the two spurs, making a draught-proof wooden screen across the end of the hall, broken only by two gaps for people to pass through. In Tudor times these openings became doors to what was known as the 'screens passage'.

Bricks were more commonly used by this time, though they were of coarse texture and unevenly fired; they had the advantage of providing a less expensive interior facing than stone for the ordinary householder.

Inevitably, a chimney that was badly constructed would harbour a good deal of soot on projections, and it was unlikely to be cleaned satisfactorily with the universally used holly branch; so the early wall fireplaces, though an improvement on the central hearth, were still likely to be smoky. Moreover, the waste of heat up the chimney must have been enormous.

It is difficult to understand why the idea of the hood which channelled the smoke up the flue was abandoned, unless in their anxiety to become more sophisticated people were positively looking for change, a new look for the interior of the room. Without the hood, in adverse weather conditions the smoke must have billowed out into the room and caused almost as much inconvenience as the smoke from the old central fire.

In due course an effort was often made to overcome this drawback by adding a band of leather or some similar material below the mantel-shelf, and still later the mantel itself was lowered.

3

Tudor Craftsmanship

The Tudor period, covering the latter part of the fifteenth century and the first half of the sixteenth, was an age of rapid development and great change in England. The wool trade was booming and a new comfortably-off middle class emerged with a great desire to better themselves.

The result was that by the end of the fifteenth century a great number of houses in the middle category were built, between those of the wealthy nobleman and the humble cottager. In new buildings the fireplace ranked as the most important feature. Built against the side wall of the hall its inclusion became assured in all but the very poorest houses.

Central fires were finally abolished and now that the need for a smoke outlet in the roof was removed, it became possible to put a ceiling across the upper part of the hall, halving its height and conserving the heat, while at the same time providing a second and even a third storey. A great two-storeyed chimney stack was built to serve the hall and a chamber above it.

It was discovered also that the fireplace need no longer be confined to an outside wall, but could be recessed within the thickness of a wall, with the flue rising vertically, thereby producing two smaller rooms in the space occupied by the large draughty hall. On the whole, the siting of the chimney stack depended a good deal on local tradition and the

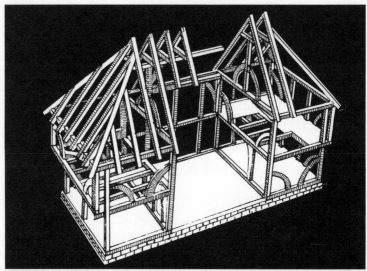

7 (a) working model of Eyhorne Manor, Kent (c1420), showing the original central hall open to the roof and (b) the insertion of a great central chimney stack serving fireplaces on two floors after the hall was subdivided (c1611)

materials available, as well as the date when the improvement was made.

In the manor house the hall fireplace usually backed on to a cross passage, so that it was as sheltered as possible. A novel and economic development was to put the fireplace, or possibly two, back to back on the axis of the house, with the chimney stack emerging through the ridge of the roof. This new arrangement can be seen in many old timber-frame houses that have been restored, their construction being flexible enough to take additions and alterations without affecting the essential framework.

An example of this kind of fireplace insertion can be seen at Eyhorne Manor, Hollingbourne, Kent. The present owners took immense trouble to restore the house to its original early fifteenth-century state, and during investigations found four different fireplaces before the great open Tudor one was exposed. It was a typical hall house of the period, originally having a central fire in the hall open to the rafters, the fireplace and chimney stack being added almost 200 years later. The fireplace opening was 10ft deep and 8ft wide and swallowed up almost half the space of the hall. A working model devised by the present owner, Derek Simmons, shows the various stages of construction very clearly and demonstrates the logical and simple methods the early builders employed.

It is now restored to its former state, a magnificent open brick fireplace, with a wide chimney tapering off at the first floor. Huge logs burn in the hearth, and a spit, skillet, bellows and other implements remind us of its central part in domestic life.

At about the same time as the fireplace was installed, a smoke bay was built leading off the flue, to be used for smoking bacon; previously this had to be cured anywhere in the room where it could conveniently hang. It is a very big bay, 16ft wide, 8ft deep and 30ft high. Nine nails for hanging carcases on the walls are visible, but from the size many more could have been accommodated. In order that visitors may see it to advantage Mr Simmons built a gallery about halfway up.

From this time forward we see a steady progression towards more comfort in the home; as a fireplace was always required, designs that could be adapted for all needs and all pockets were developed. The

Dissolution of the Monasteries left a great number of masons with time on their hands. They were often called on to build fireplaces in stone, with flues to carry off the smoke, and houses of traditional late medieval design placed the hall fireplace with its back to the cross passage, or screens passage, the fireplace itself becoming a huge cavernous recess dominating the entire wall.

At first it had a four-centred arch over it, the jambs chamfered and stopped high up with a decorative feature such as a Tudor rose, a fern leaf or a shield carved in the spandrels. This was a common treatment for fireplace openings in medieval, Tudor and early Jacobean times. The chamfer, formed by cutting off a square edge at an equal angle to each face, could be hollow or moulded. The fireplace was framed in stone and lined with stone or brick, sometimes with herringbone-pattern brickwork, with great fire-dogs in the hearth to keep the logs from rolling out into the room. A typical early fireplace of this type is seen in Wolsey's rooms at Hampton Court Palace, and it is surprisingly simple.

A much more elaborate form of decoration is seen on the fireplaces from Tattershall Castle, plaster casts of which are in the Victoria & Albert Museum. The carved ornament and heraldic work represent the peak of Gothic fireplace design and ornamentation, evidence of the fine craftsmanship of those days. The building was erected by Lord Treasurer Cromwell between 1433 and 1455, and the purse which is seen in the panels refers to the office he held.

The four-centred arch was just right for the fireplace, and the deep lintels that were necessary to span the wide openings presented a splendid opportunity for the Gothic craftsman mason to exercise his skill. Sometimes there was a kind of mantelpiece, supported by a cornice, and in the houses of the wealthy the space above the mantel would be filled by a tapestry, specially designed for the position and called a 'chimneypiece'; or it might be a tablet of wood, elaborately carved or painted with coats of arms, shields, floral emblems or fabulous scenes. Whatever form it took, it was designed as a focal point, to emphasise the importance of the fireplace. It was not necessarily a fixture; like the wall hangings and the glass windows, it might be taken down during the owner's absence.

When in the early sixteenth century it became the custom to panel the walls, often to ceiling height, the space above the fireplace was also panelled and enriched with armorial bearings. Henry VIII spent large sums of money on treating his royal apartments in this way.

The masons were able to cut well-dressed stones at this period, giving a good clean appearance that lent itself to carving and decoration, and some remarkably fine and delicate work was done on these early fireplaces, demonstrating very ably the Gothic principle of 'ornamented construction'.

In its simplest form the fireplace had a massive mantel beam, hewn from good English oak, sometimes chamfered, sometimes squared off, the marks of the adze left on, and this treatment has always seemed right for rugged 'hole in the wall' fireplaces; nothing has ever satisfactorily replaced it. The beam was used as a lintel resting on jambs of stone or brick, or sometimes it was framed into the main timbers of a building; it could be as much as 10ft wide.

Before the end of the reign of Henry VIII bricklayers were coming over from Flanders and bringing their skills with them, and so it became possible for the yeoman to have a copy of the stone fireplace in the lord's house built in brick. This, and the general improvement in social conditions, soon brought these simple recessed fireplaces within the reach of the common people and they became the most important feature in the home of cottager and yeoman alike, the centre of family life.

Cottages in the vernacular Tudor style survive in most towns and villages of Kent, and many small houses built around 1450 show evidence of having the hall ceiled and open fireplaces inserted at a later date, some having bread ovens of brick and clay built into the walls and opening out at the side of the fireplace. In smaller houses, where space was more limited, they were made to project beyond the outside walls and carried their own roofs.

It is not uncommon to find a 'luck token' in the form of old shoes, gloves, coins or other small items during restoration, as they were often deposited at a time of some major domestic event or improvement.

They sometimes help to date a house, or at least part of it. At Eyhorne Manor, Hollingbourne, Kent, a child's shoe and a human bone were found buried in the chimney. They were probably put there in the first place to encourage fertility. Odd finds like this give one a further fascinating glimpse into the strange superstitions and folklore surrounding the fireplace.

These simple, homely fireplaces became an integral part of the life of the farmhouse and cottage, the chimney corner providing ample space for all the family occupations carried on in the living-room.

They were indeed almost like self-contained kitchens, as much as 10ft wide in some yeomen's houses, 6 to 7ft wide in cottages and half as deep, occupying almost the whole of one wall. Often they had seats within, as well as a bar for pothangers and for the suspension of a spit, an adaptable iron crane or stock pot, and a great variety of cooking utensils, all of them showing in some way the skill and the artistry of the smith. A recess in the wall near the hearth, known as the salt box, kept the salt dry and another smaller cavity, with a door to it, would be the spice cupboard. If there was no smoke bay, flitches of bacon were hung in the wide mouth of the chimney, to be cured by smoke from the wood fire.

In some houses iron bars in the form of steps were built into the chimneys for the boys who had to climb up to sweep them.

A very old feature that was probably in existence in crofters' cottages in Tudor times was the cloam-oven. Built at the right-hand side of the open hearth at shoulder level, it had a stone floor and dome-shaped roof. When it was to be used for baking, a wood fire was laid on the floor to heat it, and when a high enough temperature had been reached, the burning embers were scooped out and bread or oatcakes baked in it on a bakestone or 'backstone'. The entrance to the oven was sealed with a large stone or stones. The principle was almost the same as that used by the people of the New Stone Age with their cooking holes outside their huts. Bake ovens of this kind are commonplace along the Scottish Border Country and in some Welsh houses even today, but they are invariably fitted with iron doors. The cloam ovens are much earlier, though it is difficult to discover just how far they go back.

So for the average person in Tudor times the cooking was done in the living-room and the great open hearth served a multitude of purposes; but in the houses of the nobility the kitchen fireplace was a feature in its own right, far removed from the lord's dining-hall – so far, indeed, that one wonders how the nobility ever managed to get any hot food at all. The Great Kitchen at Hampton Court Palace provides a typical example.

It needs little imagination to visualise the great wood fires that had to be kept constantly stoked in order to roast the meat on the spits and keep the stock-pot simmering. Sometimes there were brick screens to shield the boy or man who was kept busy turning the spit by hand, the power being supplied by a weight that the boy, the skip-jack, had to skip to wind up. Smaller houses had no such mechanical aids, but in many old Welsh farmhouses there exists an apparatus for turning a large roast of meat over a fire, and attached to it is a cage-like treadmill. A Welsh corgi dog fits easily into this and it has been suggested that turning spits was originally the dog's main work – though there once existed a breed of dog called the turnspit.

4

The Classical Style

From the days of Henry VIII there had been a trend towards a more classical style of architecture, though it did not at first affect fireplace design to any great extent. The social and religious upheavals of this reign weakened many old traditions and opened the way for new ideas as Elizabethan architecture gradually merged into Jacobean.

By the last half of the sixteenth century and the beginning of the seventeenth the influence of the Renaissance movement in England was slowly making itself felt until finally it supplanted medieval ways and ideas. It became fashionable for the nobility and gentry to send their sons to Italy and not unnaturally they brought back foreign ideas about design. Their strange, extravagant tastes bewildered English craftsmen. The members of the new aristocracy were the wealthy merchants, and they, too, were convinced that the best came from Italy. The craftsmen had no choice but to meet their demands.

It was nothing new for foreign influence to affect English craftsmen, for they had already been compelled to absorb French and Flemish ideas. The classic orders of the Italian Renaissance which the architects wished to introduce into England were now conformed to by the craftsmen to a certain degree, but in the main they based their ideas of the Roman orders and their characteristic ornament on copy books. The Flemish pattern books, in particular, with their lavish use of strap-work, had a very marked effect on the work of English builders and woodworkers, though it was slow to affect fireplaces.

The influence of the French and Italian craftsmen introduced to England by Henry VIII and Cardinal Wolsey first began to be seen in the ornamentation of Gothic features with Renaissance detail; thus it was in the spandrels and mouldings of the Tudor arched·fireplace that we first notice this change of character.

A notable exception to this is seen in the famous design by Hans Holbein, now in the British Museum. This artist won the favour of Henry VIII and his painting anticipates the Renaissance style at the peak of its development. It introduces the strange form of the caryatid – a female figure supporting an entablature in place of a column – which was to be a favourite feature for many years to come.

The Elizabethan age was one of lavish hospitality, when owners of great houses vied with each other in their attempts to make their homes fit for the Queen to visit, should she pass their way during a royal progress. Many great houses have their 'Queen Elizabeth bedrooms' where the Queen is purported to have slept for a night, and not infrequently an inscription above the fireplace commemorates this visit. At Knebworth House, for instance, a panel above the stone fireplace in a bedroom records a visit in 1588. It was another example of the importance which the people of this age attached to the fireplace. The fire, with its friendly, cheerful blaze which was the central point of hospitality became also the focal point of decoration, to which all eyes would turn on entering a room.

The Elizabethans, with their strong sense of theatre, understood this very well and the chimneypiece became a magnificent setting for a roaring open fire and, incidentally, the most conspicuous field on which to display the Royal coat of arms. From being simply 'a chimney cloth set in a frayme of wood', as it was in medieval times, it became a towering structure framing the hearth and soaring above it in tiers of stone, wood or plaster, up to the ceiling, on which sculptors, artists, woodcarvers and, later, architects, displayed their skill. It became, in fact, the central feature of applied art in all important rooms.

In the homes of the wealthy it was emphasised by decoration such as a coat of arms – the Royal one taking pride of place – shields or floral emblems, carved in stone, wood or brick as an overmantel. Sometimes there was a kind of mantelpiece supported by a cornice. Chimney-pieces were often pretentious but not always beautiful. The Flemish and German craftsmen reaching England at this time seemed to have an endless variety of designs and motifs at their finger tips, but some chimneypieces of this period were crude and too richly embellished for English taste, overloaded with ornamentation on every inch of surface, be it in wood, stone or marble.

One of the main characteristics of Elizabethan and Jacobean decoration is the use of strapwork, a bas-relief geometrical design of interlacing straps, often with a sprinkling of lozenges, diamonds and ovals to emphasise it. This, with a mixture of emblematic figures, classical foliage, panels and tapering pilasters resulted in an incompatible mixture of Gothic and Renaissance ideas that could become overpowering.

The Gothic principle of 'ornamented construction' was deserted, in that the more elaborate chimneypieces of this period do not form an integral part of the structure and are not always in harmony with their surroundings. This may be because they were the work of a man whose responsibility rested there. It was not until much later that they became incorporated into an architect's plans and were seen as an essential part of the interior design of a room.

Generally speaking, a fireplace was designed in two stages, in the form of architectural orders, occupying the height of a room. In his book *The English Fireplace,* Shuffrey describes them thus: 'In the lower stage, coupled columns standing on pedestals on each side of the fireplace support an entablature, the cornice of which forms the mantelshelf. In the upper, a lighter order is used, the place of the columns being frequently taken by caryatids – the lower extremities being merged into a pillar. Often on the heads of these figures rest baskets of fruit or flowers which form the capitals for the upper entablatures to rest upon.' The space over the mantelshelf between the upper columns was frequently filled with the arms of the reigning sovereign, or of the noble owner, sometimes enhanced with the addition of gold or colour. The effect was not so artistic where the discipline of an heraldic subject was lacking.

8 Stone chimneypiece in the Great Hall, Burghley House

Materials and design were so varied, indeed, that it becomes difficult
to classify them. Some show marked regional characteristics, and these
may have been the work of a group of craftsmen in adjacent counties.
It is interesting to see and compare a number of early Elizabethan
fireplaces, and fortunately there are still a great many left, particularly
in stately homes.

Stone was the favourite material in the early part of this period. In the
Great Hall of Burghley House, Stamford, there is an imposing chimneypiece of stone rising to the height of 20ft and of proportionate width.
In the centre of the tapering overpiece is a bas-relief of the arms of the
first Lord Burghley, Lord High Treasurer to Queen Elizabeth I, by
whom the house was built. The grate is equally imposing, made of
burnished steel, with massive lions at each corner, supporting the Cecil
arms and those of Poyntz and Montague. The fender is also of pierced
burnished steel; the fencings of the grate are ormolu and are inlaid with
blue and white Indian porcelain tiles (page 39).

It is a dignified composition, worthy of its setting in this fine Elizabethan Great Hall, its design resisting the temptation to be over-lavish
with decoration.

In some early examples of Jacobean stone chimneypieces, one order
encloses the whole composition, both mantel and overmantel. There is a
striking example at Loseley Park (Surrey) in the drawing-room. The
house was built by Sir William More in 1562–8 and is full of associ-
ations with Queen Elizabeth. The fireplace is in fact carved from a solid
block of clunch chalk, quarried at Melbourne, Cambridgeshire. It is
after a Holbein design, with elaborate caryatids in the upper stage. The
spaces over the shelf are filled with the heraldic bearings of the More
family and in the strapwork in the centre panel are some grotesque little
faces with their tongues sticking out, supposedly to keep the evil spirits
away. Such intricate carving would demand great skill in wood, and in
chalk is a fantastic achievement.

The great rectangular fire-opening caters for big log fires, but it has
been filled in with an arched front at some later date, probably to
combat a smoky chimney.

Loseley also supplies a good example of the Elizabethan passion for

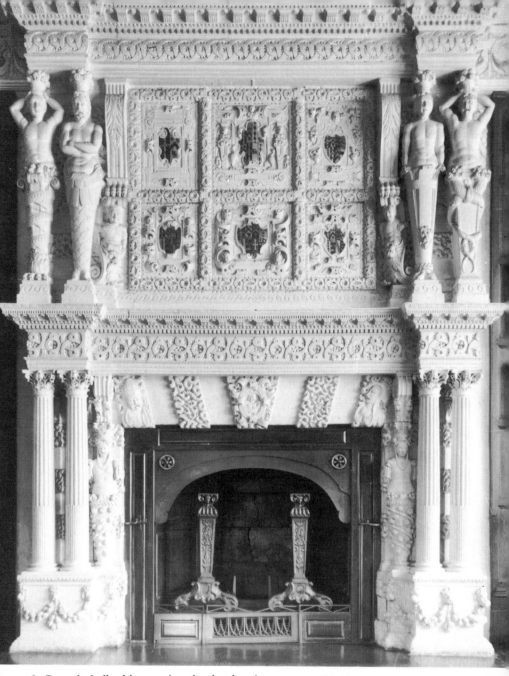

9 Carved chalk chimneypiece in the drawing-room at Loseley Park, Surrey

heraldry. The chimneypiece in the dining-room bears the family emblems of moorhens, cockatrices and mulberry trees; a central panel bears shields each side of a mulberry tree, with a Latin epigram meaning 'The More family, like the mulberry tree, shall endure for a long time, but the individual Mores, like the fruit, shall perish more quickly.' In this chimneypiece caryatids take the place of columns in the lower stage, and the fruit-basket capitals are replaced by trusses resting on the heads of the figures without any horizontal moulding.

Both of these Loseley fireplaces have their original firedogs.

Of a different character is the massive Caen stone fireplace in the Great Hall of Charterhouse, London, which was inserted about a century after Henry VIII built the hall, then open to the roof. From its decoration, one assumes it was put in by Sir Thomas Sutton, who bought the place from the Duke of Norfolk and founded the Hospital in 1610. It bears the Sutton arms and crest, a talbot's head.

A massive lintel spans an opening 8ft wide and shows the lavish use of strapwork and other Flemish ornament in vogue at the time. The central cartouche over the fireplace opening is carved with a salamander in flames, a creature that was an emblem of constancy and fabled to live in fire. It is strangely prophetic here, for Charterhouse suffered severely from fire bombs in World War II – but the fireplace survived.

Above the cartouche are Sutton's arms and crest – a talbot's head – and at each end of the overmantel is a little cannon, with a keg of gunpowder and balls beside it, alluding to Sutton's long service as Master-General of the Ordnance in the North. It was not uncommon for the decoration of chimneypieces to show the profession of the owner.

The firegrate of cast iron is one of the earliest examples of a coal-burning grate. There is no reason to suppose it is not original and in this case it is also very appropriate, for Sir Thomas Sutton made his fortune by bringing coals to London. The cast-iron standards of the grate terminate in the talbot's head, following the pattern of the newels on the staircase.

The sculptors of this period, who produced such fine monuments, also worked upon chimneypieces. In Nicholas Stone's notebook, preserved in the Soane Museum, there are references to many chimney-

10 Dining-room chimneypiece at Loseley Park

11 Caen stone fireplace with sarcophagus-type grate, in the Great Hall,
Charterhouse, London

12 Elizabethan moulded stone fireplace with wall painting at Teynham, Kent

pieces he made, for which he received generous payment. It is difficult after this passage of time to attribute any particular work to him, though in the view of many historians it is unlikely that most have been destroyed. Though Stone, with Nicholas Johnson, carved Sutton's monument in the Chapel at Charterhouse, from the accounts it seems that the Caen stone fireplace in the Great Hall was the work of Edmund Kinsman, a master mason who became Master of the Masons' Company in 1635.

Stone chimneypieces of early seventeenth-century origin often bore some highly characteristic features which one seldom sees repeated. An interesting one in the Victoria & Albert Museum was taken from an old house in Norwich. It has a deep lintel finished with moulding forming a mantelshelf. The lintel is carved with gorgons' heads supported by wyverns on each side, a vase of fruit and flowers in the centre carved on a band of strapwork. The composition and details of mouldings on this chimneypiece are of a higher standard than much of the ornament of this Jacobean period.

In the smaller house the Tudor stone fireplace lingered on in the form of a four-centred arch, its importance emphasised by decoration. Restoration has uncovered some of these early fireplaces with their original wall paintings above them. Painting direct on to plaster was more expensive than painting cloth, and this kind of chimneypiece is found more in the home of the well-to-do yeoman and the nobility than in the humble cottage. It is possible that the paintings were done by itinerant artists who left little or no evidence of their identity.

Genuine examples are becoming very rare, since so many people have covered up old fireplaces instead of restoring them as they deserve. It was exciting, therefore, when in the course of restoring a fifteenth-century timber-frame house in Teynham, Kent, the owners discovered two splendid Elizabethan fireplaces with their original wall paintings above them.

The first, in an upstairs bedroom, is of moulded stone, dating from 1587. Along the lintel is a sculptured design of Tudor roses, daisies and leaves, painted in soft shades of red, ochre and green on an ochre background marbled with brown. The painting above depicts a lady

13 Elizabethan moulded brick fireplace in the Great Hall at Bumpitt, Teynham. The wall painting has been perfectly restored to the original

sitting in a chair, a book in her lap, and opposite is a picture of a man, which unfortunately suffered damage from rain when the roof was needing repair. There are traces of an inscription also, not clear enough to define, but it is assumed that the figures are portraits of former owners of the house, as this was usual in those days.

The second fireplace was discovered in the Great Hall (page 47). This one is of fine moulded brick, which had been painted with red ochre and marbled so that it is difficult to distinguish from stone at first sight. In the spandrels is the crest of the Ropers (the owners of the house in 1587), a black lion rampant holding a gold coronet on a silver ground. The fireplace opening is 8ft wide, and there is still some of the original herringbone brickwork behind a cast-iron fireback dated 1588. The firedogs, of about the same date, have a design of hammer and tongs on their standards. Above is an exceptionally fine wall painting of the Royal coat of arms, supported by the English lion and the Welsh dragon of the Tudors, with a free-flowing design of fruit and birds in the background.

This fireplace was hidden behind a bolection moulding surround in pine, painted dark brown, in the centre of which was a kitchen range. The wall painting had been limewashed over and the date 1688 scratched on it; it took a winter's painstaking work to restore the whole to its Elizabethan splendour.

In this colourful, flamboyant age, painting on any surface became a fine art. On a more magnificent scale, and in a different idiom, is the painted chimneypiece in the Great Chamber at Charterhouse. Though blackened and blistered, the painting miraculously survived the fire of 1941 and has since been perfectly restored (page 49).

The fireplace opening is framed by the typical four-centred Tudor arch in stone, but the painted decoration was probably put in by the Duke of Norfolk in the latter part of the sixteenth century when Charterhouse was a private residence and this was his drawing-room. This is evident from his heraldry and the motto of the Howards displayed on the ceiling.

The chimneypiece is richly and beautifully coloured, with a lavish use of gold for the groundwork, and the arabesques are graceful and

14 Sixteenth-century painted chimneypiece in the Great Chamber at Charterhouse

delicate. The royal arms of James I appear in the oval of the centre panel, and the shield and initials of Sutton in the panel below it. It seems that this work was added at a later date, for the name of Rowland Buckett, limner, was found at the back of the oval panel, and he evidently made these alterations and did some repairs in 1626. Set in medallions about the oval are the emblems of the four Evangelists, with portraits of the twelve Apostles on the columns. In the panels below the columns are paintings of the Annunciation and the Last Supper, beautifully detailed, and between the columns at the side of the fireplace opening are emblematic paintings set in cartouches. These last appear to be by a different hand, very likely that of Rowland Buckett who, it is recorded, received £50 from the governors of the Charterhouse for his work.

The Elizabethans also had a great fondness for colouring and embellishing their chimneypieces with a 'posy' – that is to say, a moral maxim, a pithy saying or a rhyme, inscribed decoratively over the fireplace and sometimes round the frieze. This moral exhortation was usually executed by a craftsman from the Netherlands, but it was not always so. Thomas Tusser, the Elizabethan versifier, has suggestions for bedchamber posies that warn the guest how to behave, in much the same way that a seaside landlady might have done it earlier in the twentieth century.

It is a pity that so many of these quaint inscriptions have been lost through ignorance of their existence or meaning, or that 'modernisation' which in every age has been responsible for destruction; but we still have old prints, records and accounts as a valuable source of information.

In general, local material was used for fireplaces but at this time there was a vogue for imported coloured marbles for decorative chimneypieces. The most important designs in marble consisted of two stages, as already described in the chalk chimneypiece at Loseley Park. Sometimes a geometric arrangement of marble filled the space usually taken by an heraldic subject, or some elaborately sculptured allegorical or scriptural subjects were chosen, and these were popular in wood, stone or marble. Some alabaster was also used. There is an interesting series of chimneypieces at Bolsover Castle, Derbyshire, which illustrate the

15 Marble and alabaster hooded fireplace in the north-east room on the first floor of the Keep, Bolsover Castle

use of alabaster with stone. The one on page 51 has a projecting hood sloping back to the main wall face, which is of dressed stone. The design, attributed to Huntingdon Smithson, was probably inspired by Italian work but the classical enrichments are applied in an unusual way. The detail on some of the brackets is also unusual and represents some very fine work (page 53). All the Bolsover fireplaces are varied in plan, some being built in the angles of the rooms and having conical hoods, and some being square or part octagon.

In districts where stone was not easily obtainable, brick was used and the chimneypieces were made of oak. To protect the woodwork from the heat of the fire an inner lining of stone was used, the jambs and lintel either being plainly moulded or richly ornamented.

There are not many of these interesting fireplaces left intact, except in museums, and the Victoria & Albert has a fine one set up in a panelled room. It was removed from the Old Palace, Bromley-by-Bow, when the building was demolished. The fireplace dates from 1606, and the broad stone lintel is elaborately carved with birds, beasts and reptiles. The oak overmantel is carved with the Royal Arms in the place of honour, with the symbolic figures of Peace and Plenty each side. To a large extent, it reflects the influence of Flemish architectural pattern books and was probably originally painted in gold and other colours.

A further example of the same period is seen from an old house in Lime Street, London, that was demolished in 1875. The stone chimney-piece, of early seventeenth-century origin, has a carved oak overmantel in a formal strapwork design that was probably Germanic in origin. The jambs and lintel are of moulded stone.

Wood chimneypieces became commonplace in Jacobean times. There were some very elaborately carved oak ones of Renaissance character, following Italian rather than Flemish models, and in nearly all of them the arms of Queen Elizabeth have pride of place. The downward tapering pilaster is seen in many forms, decorated by strap carving, reeds, flutes, bosses and nailheads, sometimes exaggerated, sometimes graceful and in proportion with the human figure.

A typical early Jacobean fireplace makes good use of columns, panelling and ornament, but the Gothic tradition remains in the Tudor

16 Detail of fireplace bracket in the second floor room over the Heaven
Chamber, Little Castle, Bolsover Castle

arch framing the fireplace opening, with chamfèrs stopped high up.

Doubtless it was the influx of foreign craftsmen that stimulated the
English workers to develop and improve their own designs, and the
result was gradually seen in a more formalised treatment of chimneypieces, though details were still apt to be crude at times. Many of these
more restrained designs are to be found in small manor houses or those
of master weavers, built at the height of their prosperity. Sometimes a
chimneypiece was made more interesting by the addition of box or
ebony inlay to the panels. One of this type is in the Oak Room of the
Ancient House, Ipswich (accessible to the public, since it is now a
bookshop). The sides of the open fireplace and the panelling of the

overmantel, inlaid in a fanciful design with wood of a lighter colour, have a fine effect in contrast with the almost black oak. In the centre is a bas-relief of the arms and crest of the Sparrowe family, former owners of the house, with a monogram and the date 1603.

Of the various styles in use during this period, some were almost flat, with only very slight projections and with caryatids dividing the panels. A favourite form was a square within a cross, or a semicircular arch on pilasters, which provided a way of filling in compartments. Sometimes these compartments were filled with a Biblical story, as in the Queen's Room at Loseley Park where the story of the Good Samaritan is carved in four panels above the fireplace.

Charles Lamb, in his reminiscences of Blakesware House, speaks of the story of the Babes in the Wood being carved on a chimneypiece. There are many similar interesting subjects to be discovered in old houses.

5

The Influence of the Architect

Early Renaissance work displayed a certain lack of harmony and over-enthusiasm where decoration was concerned, but the dawn of the Anglo-Classic period in the latter half of the seventeenth century brought considerable changes in architectural character which had a direct effect on the design of fireplaces.

Traditional forms began to merge into classical at about the time the individual architect came on the scene; here was a man who could see the design of a house as a whole with all the component parts linked together in harmony. The medieval impression of straggling 'bittiness' was no longer tolerated in houses of quality.

Much of this change was indirectly due to the great Italian architect, Andrea Palladio, whose influence on Inigo Jones was considerable. When Jones visited Italy he became wholly converted to the classical concept of architecture. He was in fact the first to introduce the pure Italian Renaissance style to Britain; this 'Palladian' was a scholarly classical style, where the 'Orders of Architecture' were used to give importance and dignity to a composition, and proportion was the dominant factor. To achieve this object it was necessary to supply full-size details of the various parts and so the practice of the professional architect had begun.

In chimneypieces regular classical forms took the place of some of the more extravagant designs that had gone before. The fireplace, with open dog-grate, after Jacobean models, was often richly treated with columns, while the overmantel had carved festoons with coat-of-arms, the whole design being in harmony with the treatment of the walls.

English craftsmen were not yet accustomed to this novel style of architecture. There had been much dalliance with Renaissance decorative motifs in Tudor times, but otherwise they had usually, till now, contributed their own decorative features according to the ancient patterns inherited from their forefathers. So to a certain extent Inigo Jones found himself handicapped by a lack of experienced craftsmen. Wren was the one who was to profit by their improvement half a century later.

Writing in his *Sketch Book* in 1615, after he had left Italy, Jones says, 'In all inventions of capricious ornaments one must first design the ground, or the thing, plain, as it is for use, and on that vary it, adorn it. Compose it with decorum according to the use and the order it is of. . . .' He deplores heaping capricious ornaments on facades at the expense of their design, but 'in ornaments of chimneypieces or in the inner parts of houses these compositions are of necessity to be used.' We can see this use of 'capricious ornament' very clearly on some of his famous chimneypieces in many stately homes and public buildings today.

In spite of hindrances from many quarters, Inigo Jones produced some of the most beautiful and memorable work of his age. His designs for chimneypieces embracing the whole height of a room reflect his wide knowledge of classical art. His early training as an artist and masque-producer can be seen in his liking for passing drapery in and out of mouldings, giving them a theatrical effect.

The type of marble mantel he introduced started a fashion which was followed throughout the eighteenth century. Some of the most famous of Inigo Jones' chimneypieces are to be seen at Wilton House, Salisbury, home of the Earls of Pembroke for over 400 years. Seven rooms of the south front survive practically as Jones and his architect nephew, John Webb, left them, a group of incomparable beauty.

The double and single cube rooms (so called because one is double the size of the other which is a perfect 'cube') are indeed the most famous seventeenth-century apartments in all England, with chimneypieces to equal them in importance.

17 Inigo Jones' chimneypiece in the Double Cube Room at Wilton House, Salisbury

In the Double Cube Room, which was specially designed to take the family portraits by Van Dyck, is a fine white marble chimneypiece, with an overpiece of wood, painted and partly gilded, to harmonise with the rest of the room (page 57). Front and side consoles have festoons of fruit hanging from voluted sides, and a broken pediment over the centre tablet contains a cartouche with the Pembroke cipher with coronet. A portrait group of the three eldest children of Charles I and his French wife, Henrietta Maria, occupies the central space in a richly carved frame surrounded by drapery, having the Prince of Wales' feathers in the centre. The figures of Peace and Plenty stand one on each side in front of fluted Corinthian columns which support a rich entablature. The splendid crowning pediment is opened for a crowned shield, with reclining figures on its curved sides after the style of Michelangelo.

A specially designed grate, with coved cheeks and a marble hearth of geometrical design, complete this beautiful composition.

There is also in this room a Louis XVI Royal cheval glass fire-screen with the monogram of Queen Marie Antoinette of France above it.

An equally good example of Jones' master hand is seen in the colonnade room, formerly the state bedroom, where full advantage has been taken of a projecting chimney breast. The pediment works in with the cornice supremely well and the central cartouche is poised over Salvi's picture of the Madonna. A third important chimneypiece on these lines is in the corner room, where gilt dragons on the slopes of the pediment form an impressive feature. In the central space above the mantel is a portrait of Prince Rupert of the Rhine painted by Gerard von Honthorst in the early seventeenth century. The carved and gilded frame is surrounded by the festoons and draperies so typical of Inigo Jones' designs.

These Wilton chimneypieces are of Carrara marble, carved in Italy and brought over by the first Earl of Pembroke. The style of carving bears this out. All the chimneypieces in the state rooms are well worth detailed study in order to grasp the significance of the work of this great master, with the new grandeur and classical beauty that he brought to fireplace design.

Inigo Jones attained the highest architectural post in England as surveyor-general to Charles I; he built the Queen's House, Greenwich (1616–35), and a number of other important houses. Sir William Chambers, referring to chimneypieces in his *Civil Architecture,* wrote: 'I believe we may justly consider Inigo Jones as the first who arrived at any degree of perfection in this material branch of the art.' His designs also inspired many gifted sculptors of the day, who spent almost all their time in carving these magnificent chimneypieces.

What we know of the work of John Webb, nephew and pupil of Inigo Jones, shows a similar style to that of his uncle, with heavy swags of fruit and foliage predominating, and bold pediments to add importance to the composition. Both Jones and Webb had a particular liking for the palm-tree decoration, which they used frequently. It was subsequently much copied by Georgian architects. In Vardy's *Some Designs of Inigo Jones,* 1657, was a very fanciful design for a chimneypiece for a Jacobean palace, with reversed scrolls of palm branches and draperies for the main decorative theme.

There is much repetition of pattern in seventeenth-century designs because the architects so frequently copied each other. In addition, they very often left the choice of decorative motif to the craftsmen they employed, who in turn travelled around the country wherever their work took them; so it is hardly surprising that one comes across the designs of a leading craftsman over and over again in various buildings.

The basic conception of a chimneypiece at this time seems to have been a solid affair heavily framed in marble, with deep curly mouldings and possibly a pediment on top; stuccoists and joiners kept several stock patterns which they reproduced as they chose, in the materials most easily available. Master masons and sculptors with a sense of line and curve produced beautiful work in costly stone and marble, and Inigo Jones must often have used the services of Nicholas Stone, then master mason to the Crown.

There were also, of course, less important chimneypieces designed in Portland or Weldon stone, or with the lower stage in stone and the upper in wood. Overmantels also continued to be made in plaster, which was more used in the early part of the seventeenth century.

There were some early examples of the use of deal for mantelshelves, instead of the traditional oak, some having mitred and broken mouldings in the formal design of the overmantel which show the influence of Inigo Jones. By this time, because of the shortage of native home-grown oak the builders were increasingly turning their attention to imported softwoods, and from now on we see more pine used for over-mantels. To quote an example, there is a particularly fine carved pinewood chimneypiece in the London Museum, dated 1635–40. It was acquired from Poyle Park House, Farnham, Surrey, the property of Sir Nicholas Woodroffe in 1582, but now demolished.

The chimneypiece towers to ceiling height above a moulded marble surround to the fire opening, and is lavishly carved with scrolls, drapery and other adornments. There are niches each side of the overpiece, each containing a casket. The pediment opening contains a similar casket, and above it all is a cartouche with painted arms (a modern addition) flanked by swags of fruit and foliage. It was once part of a panelled room and must have looked imposing *in situ*.

By the time of Inigo Jones' death in 1652 the transitional period from medieval to the classical style of architecture was virtually at an end, and England was entering on a highly civilised age of great artificiality, a state which was faithfully reflected in the different designs that were to follow.

Christopher Wren was the next great architect who influenced fire-place design, beginning what is known as the Queen Anne style. He profited to a certain degree from the experience the craftsmen had gained under Inigo Jones and followed his illustrious predecessor in designing chimneypieces that embraced the whole height of a room; but in the main his designs were his own. They were indeed different from anything that had gone before and expressed the changing moods and tastes of an age of fashion and elegance inspired by the restoration of Charles II and, as John Evelyn, the seventeenth-century diarist, puts it, 'a politer way of living'.

Added to this, the skill of English craftsmen was improving, rapidly approaching the standards of French and Netherlands workers; an English style had evolved that was less flamboyant than that of the Low

Countries, though their influence remained. Thus we see a complex of continental tastes adapted by English craftsmen.

Wren was already familiar with engineering when he turned to architecture and his taste for regular order and precision is very evident. He evolved a broad panelled style in which the chimneypiece was subordinated to the general design of a room rather than being the main focal point, as in the Elizabethan age. Nevertheless, it had a dignified effect and the style spread to humbler homes. A room panelled in its entirety may often be seen in a small manor or farmhouse; heavy wood mouldings frame the fire opening and a superstructure is dispensed with. Where it was obtainable, stone often took the place of wood.

One of the chief characteristics of Wren's fireplaces was the use of heavy architraves in bolection moulding of stone or marble around the fire opening. He also followed a fashion of placing fireplaces in corners of rooms, as may be seen at Hampton Court Palace and the Queen's House at Greenwich. John Evelyn strongly criticised this practice, saying that 'it took away from the state of greater rooms'. It certainly made it difficult for people to assemble round the fire in time-honoured way and so something of the companionable element of the fireplace was lost.

As Director of Royal Building, Wren was potentially the most important architectural figure in England. He was commissioned to plan the new palace at Hampton Court for William and Mary, the old Tudor palace not being to their taste or convenience. Work was begun in 1689 and the suites of rooms and galleries were built which now surround the Fountain Court, and it is in these State Rooms that we can see a representative collection of Wren's chimneypieces and compare their characteristics with those of other architects.

In general, he rarely provided a mantelshelf at the ordinary height and his overmantels were intended only to enrich the panelling of the room, so that though pleasing they did not always make the immediate impact that was made by Inigo Jones' work. In the King's drawing-room, above the white marble bolection fireplace surround, is an overmantel of wainscot oak with elaborate festoons, wreath and cherub

18 Wren fireplace in the King's private dressing-room, Hampton Court
Palace, with overmantel carved by Grinling Gibbons

heads carved in limewood by Grinling Gibbons. It frames a large panel portrait of Isabella, Archduchess of Austria. The fireplace itself is simple, with stone side-linings of a moulded section. Wrought andirons in front of a cast fireback on a marble hearth complete the composition.

The chimneypiece in the King's private dressing-room (page 62) is rather more elaborate, with the mantel projected forward, its cornice supplying a shelf for china, with a mirror beneath it. Mirrors in this position were just then coming into fashion, and Wren used them both at Hampton Court and Kensington Palace. The fireplace in the angle of the King's dressing-room has been given original treatment by incorporating a series of steps in the overpiece, receding to the angle of the room, to provide shelves for Queen Mary's delftware ornaments.

The grey marble chimneypiece in the Queen's Gallery is not quite in Wren's usual style. It has the characteristic bolection moulding, but above it is a mirror in a brass frame surmounted by a pair of turtle-doves billing and cooing. A bust of Venus presides over them, with garlands of flowers and reclining cupids in white marble at each side. This chimneypiece was carved by John Nost and completed for Queen Anne. It shows the sculptor at his best, his minute attention to detail making the piece extraordinarily lifelike.

John Nost's work is also to be seen in the cartoon gallery, a room specially designed by Wren to display Charles I's collection of Raphael's cartoons. Here the heavy architrave mould is of coloured marbles with a white marble bas-relief carved by Nost below the mantel. The subject is a classical one, Venus again taking central place in the design. It is a work of art, beautifully executed. It was so much appreciated that replicas of the panel have since been cast in lead. Above the chimney-piece are two large pendants of fruit and flowers carved by Grinling Gibbons, the master carver, that 'incomparable young man' discovered by John Evelyn in 1671 and brought to the notice of King Charles II and Sir Christopher Wren.

Most of the carvings of the post-Restoration period are attributed to Gibbons, though it is hardly possible that he could have done them all. His signature was an open pea-pod, and where this is seen somewhere in the carving it is genuinely his. A good deal of what is claimed to be his work must have been done by the pupils under his tutelage. Nevertheless, his beautifully executed fantasies of flowers, fruit and birds adorn some of the most famous English mansions of the seventeenth century .- Chatsworth, Burghley, Petworth and others.

It was the fashion of the day to provide a space over the chimneypiece for Gibbons' applied ornament, and Wren appears to have given him a free hand in the state apartments at Hampton Court Palace. His craftsmanship was superb, endowed with a quality of lightness and naturalism that has never been equalled. It is said that he could represent a feather in wood and he once carved a point-lace cravat in limewood for the Duke of Devonshire. He was undoubtedly a genius – the greatest of all woodcarvers.

Wren frequently used mirrors in his designs to accommodate the dandies of the day who so often wanted to look at themselves. Two of his chimneypieces in Queen Mary's gallery at Kensington Palace demonstrate this idea very well. One is in the form of an imitation window constructed with mirrors, with curtains of carved wood. In the King's gallery Wren set up a novel chimneypiece featuring a circular dial on which is painted a map of the north-west of Europe, and a pointer controlled by an iron rod connected with a vane above the roof registers the direction of the wind on the map. The ingenious device is another reminder of Wren's mechanical turn of mind.

It was nothing but the age-old desire for change which supplanted all these styles, and unaccountably Gibbons' style died with him. A copy of the French style of Louis XIV was adopted for a time, culminating in the extravagances of the Chippendale school.

One sometimes comes across an example of a chimneypiece being thrown into a recess by columns being placed on either side, as in the board room of the Admiralty, Whitehall. Here fluted Corinthian pillars bound the heavy marble mantel, carved by Ripley. A wind dial is placed over the shelf and nautical instruments are a feature of the singularly beautiful carving around it, which some attribute to Grinling Gibbons, but since the building was erected after Gibbons' death it is more likely to have been by one of his pupils.

During the seventeenth century fireplaces in chambers became much

19 Chimneypiece in the boardroom of the Admiralty, Whitehall, with nautical instruments featured in the carving

more common, though it is doubtful if they were used except in cases of illness. M. W. Barley, in his book *The House and Home,* comments on a stone fireplace in a chamber of a house at Northop, Flintshire, which is narrower than would be found in a hall or kitchen. The stonework has been blackened to match the iron range which was inserted about 1800. What was called a range in the seventeenth century was simply a box to hold coal.

In the yeoman farmhouse the capacious fireplace changed little, since it had to be amply equipped for cooking for a large number of farm hands. The front of the fireplace was flanked by heavy stone or brick supports which carried the great chimney beam from which the wide flue was gathered back. Behind this, it was recessed for shelving, or seats, with arm rests and a box for salt in the thick rear wall. In the Devonshire 'front chimney' house there was also a small fire window in the corner near the front door, from which visitors could be seen.

It was a time of revival for almost everyone, and chimneys had become a powerful status symbol, indicating the number of fireplaces a home possessed. Few people would be willing to give them up. Perhaps this was the underlying reason why the Government, hard pressed by Charles II's demands for money, put a tax on hearths in 1662. Understandably, it was one of the most unpopular taxes ever levied. With the exception of small cottages, all houses were charged at the rate of two shillings for every hearth, fire or stove. The tax yielded £200,000 a year and it was voted to the Crown for ever.

It did not affect the wealthy to any great extent, but it was a heavy imposition on small house owners; when William III was on his journey to London, scores of his new subjects met him and begged to be relieved of this burden. William, seeing that it 'was very grievous to the people' abolished the tax and it was subsequently repealed after having been in force for a little over twenty-five years.

6

Georgian Elegance and the Adam Style

The Georgian age – around 1714 to 1830 – was, on the whole, one of elegance and refinement, when a substantial middle class was emerging and the 'man of taste' came to the fore. Architecture became, in a sense, a 'copy-book' art in that the new builders were adapting designs from the published works of the great architects. The first speculative builders made their appearance in London and other important cities and great numbers of unpretentious houses sprang up. There were also many houses built in the grand style, designed by architects and planned with an eye to the future.

In the early part of the eighteenth century many of these big houses were designed in the Baroque manner with large ponderous chimney-pieces, their marble mantels surrounded by elaborate wood overmantels, painted, with a central panel made to take a picture.

With the retirement of Wren and the death of Grinling Gibbons the effect of the wainscoted room and chimneypiece was lost. A classical form of architecture after the Palladian style, revived by William Kent and others, began to be admired again, the favourite decoration for chimneypieces in big houses being a 'tabernacle' form, composed of columns, entablature and pediment.

Kent's designs were always on the grand scale, his treatment bold and massive, but it must be remembered that they were for houses that were monumental in conception. That Kent was not always sure of his proportions is demonstrated in the veined white marble chimneypiece in the cupola room at Kensington Palace. The fireplace opening, though tall, appears very small by comparison with the overpiece towering above it. It has on it, however, a fine bas-relief by the sculptor Michael Rysbrack, showing a Roman marriage. The caryatid support which was used so freely during the early Renaissance was also revived to a certain extent, and the appearance of carved drapery in different forms is reminiscent of Inigo Jones.

A chimneypiece of marble, wood and plaster, partly gilded, in the Victoria & Albert Museum provides an interesting example of this period. It is one of a pair originally made for the picture gallery in Northumberland House, Strand, demolished in the nineteenth century. It is English work, about 1750, probably by Benjamin Carter. The marble entablature is supported by classical figures with cherubs and an eagle in the centre panel. The overmantel, which formerly contained a full-length portrait, has two strange sphinxes on the shelf, with caryatids at the sides surmounted by an open pediment containing a cartouche ornamented with a floral festoon. It is ornate and heavy looking, compared with Wren's work.

We meet this kind of chimneypiece in a mixture of materials surprisingly often in early eighteenth-century houses, with a fireplace opening surrounded by marble, with plaster mouldings outside the surround and plaster overmantels containing pictures. Sometimes instead of a picture there would be a medallion of some classical subject.

By the beginning of the eighteenth century marble chimneypieces had become a trade article, but designs were many and varied. English art patrons as well as architects were studying Classic and Renaissance architecture in Italy, collecting a vast number of antiquities and works of art. It is not surprising that the end result was the introduction of a medley of styles, some pleasing, some too ornate and overdone. Eventually a purer classical style found favour and gained a great following under the influence of that remarkable family of architects, the Adams.

William Adam, father of the famous brothers John, Robert, James and William, was described in his obituary as 'King's mason – a celebrated architect'. He advised Sir John Clark on the design of 'Mavisbank', Edinburgh, which included a two-tier marble chimneypiece, the upper tier to contain a mirror in a marble frame and finished with a marble astragal – a small half-round moulding. This also became a popular style in England, but it was left for his sons to create their own inimitable style and their simple, classic designs are still being reproduced today – enjoying a great revival in Georgian-style houses.

It was the second son, Robert, who was responsible for what has ever since been known as the Adam style, an all-embracing scheme of decoration which brought every part of a room into harmony by the repetition of a motif. Thus his chimneypieces were not so much a focal point as part of the general design of an interior, albeit an important one.

Robert Adam studied in Italy from 1754 to 1758 and was completely won over to the classical ideal. On his return to England, the rococo style was waning in popularity and his ambition to introduce a new concept of classical architecture was timely. He considered some of Inigo Jones' Palladian models 'absurd compositions' and out of proportion for a private house. He admired Roman architecture, with its qualities of 'delicacy, gaiety, grace and beauty', and these he endeavoured to transmit to his own work, with marked success.

For his best chimneypieces he used white statuary marble, with yellow sienna and verde-antique for inlays. He made free use of scrolls and foliage, rams' heads, sphinxes, candelabra, urns and vases as subjects for decoration, in the Greek rather than the Roman style, but his designs were always symmetrical, of good proportion and with a quality of grace and lightness that singles them out from all others of his time.

Adam's chimneypieces nearly always ended with the shelf, but in some of his designs large mirrors in gilt wooden frames form an overpiece in the light style that is seen in Pompeian wall decoration.

While in Italy the Adam brothers were assisted by Pergolesi, an expert in classical ornamentation, who came back to England to work with them. There are certain characteristic features of their work which are unmistakable, such as the elongated vase and the central tablet with a subject from the classics. They also made use of the 'orders' with detached columns, and examples of the Doric and Ionic orders in statuary marble against a background of coloured marble demonstrate

20 Robert Adam's early style in the drawing-room at Osterley Park. The same ornament is used in the fireplace, the frieze and above the bookcases

their flair for creating beauty without heaviness.

The devotee of Robert Adam cannot do better than to visit Osterley Park, Middlesex (now National Trust), which Adam undertook to remodel in 1761, just three years after his return from Italy. He took nineteen years to complete it, so it is a fair illustration of his youthful work as well as that of his maturer years.

His early style is seen in the hall, library, eating-room and drawing-room, where the decorations are bold but not heavy. The same ornament is used in the frieze around the room, above the bookcases and chimney-pieces, as in the pierced-steel apron of the grates, producing complete harmony between the parts.

In the middle period (1775–7) his style became much more refined, as may be seen in the tapestry room, the state bedroom and the Etruscan room. In his anxiety to avoid heaviness Adam resorted to ornament that was purely linear and minute in scale. When Horace Walpole visited Osterley in 1778 he described the tapestry room as 'the most superb and beautiful that can be imagined', adding 'except that he (Adam) has stuck diminutive heads in bronze, no bigger than a half-crown, into the chimneypiece's hair'. The ornaments are in fact inlaid in coloured composition and are not bronze, and the motif is repeated in a different material above the doorcases. They are undeniably small in scale, but typical of Adam's work in the middle period of his career, when he was striving for effects of great delicacy and refinement. Many of Adam's drawings are now in the Soane Museum.

It is interesting to contrast the chimneypieces in Osterley designed by Sir William Chambers with those of Adam. The marble chimney-pieces in the gallery are reputed to be designed by Chambers and probably made by Joseph Wilton, the sculptor. The caryatids supporting the shelf without the usual fruit baskets belong to an earlier period and are typical of Chambers' style. John Linnell, a prominent designer, carver and cabinetmaker during the second half of the eighteenth century, almost certainly made a chimneypiece in one of the bedrooms. Its rococo style dates it as no later than 1765.

Imitation marble was introduced during the Adam period by Italian artificers. It was known as scagliola and quickly became fashionable. At

Ham House, Surrey, there is an attractive fireplace in the Queen's closet which has panels of this imitation marble surrounding the fire opening. The design incorporates the initials J.E.L. (for John and Elizabeth Lauderdale), with a ducal coronet, a theme repeated elsewhere in the room.

At Castle Howard, Yorkshire, there is a similar use of scagliola in the surrounds to the fireplace in the Great Hall. In both of these fireplaces it is one of the earliest examples of this kind of decoration in England.

The Castle Howard chimneypiece has been aptly described as a great and gay one, quite unfamiliar in an English private house at that time. It is the work of the Italian stuccoists Bagutti and Plura, c1710, and is truly magnificent in its soaring height and gilded ornamentation. The Hall itself, Vanbrugh's first building, is 70ft high, and the chimneypiece is given an additional sense of spaciousness by arched openings above it and a pedimented niche through into the staircase spaces.

The early eighteenth century was indeed a time when many able sculptors in England were producing memorable work for chimneypieces for the great houses. Michael Rysbrack, whose work at Kensington Palace has already been mentioned, was a sculptor who came from Antwerp to England in 1720 and set up workshops in Vere Street, London. He was soon very much in demand by those members of the nobility who were building new homes or restoring old ones. Some of his finest work is to be seen at Clandon Park, Surrey, once the property of the Earl of Onslow, now National Trust.

Built by the Venetian architect Giacomi Leoni around 1730, the Great Marble Hall is among the grandest of all eighteenth-century interiors, with two magnificent marble chimneypieces by Rysbrack dominating the hall at each end. The bas-relief for the one on the south wall shows 'Sacrifice to Diana' and that on the north wall 'Sacrifice to Bacchus'. Both are lifelike portrayals set off against a background of grey marble. The one on the south wall is signed and bears a close resemblance to one in the marble parlour at Houghton Hall. In a lighter style is the chimneypiece in the green drawing-room, finished with an overmantel, with carved and gilded mouldings framing a picture by Panini.

21 Michael Rysbrack's signed chimneypiece in the Marble Hall at Clandon Park

It is noticeable that some of the fireplaces at Clandon have been built out at a later date, probably because of Leoni's failure to appreciate the rigours of the English climate, but the original chimneypieces have been retained.

Rysbrack also did some notable work in Hopetoun House, West Lothian, and in Woburn Abbey, where the carved chimneypieces in the state saloon typify his style.

John De Val also carved some beautiful chimneypieces in the state apartments at Woburn Abbey. In the room now known as the Queen's bedroom (after Queen Victoria's visit with Prince Albert in 1841) there is a superb marble chimneypiece of his, carved in 1756 at a cost of £100. De Val was responsible for many more of the Abbey's fine chimneypieces and two of his great fireplaces form the most striking feature of the long gallery. The bill records that they cost £120 each, and placed above each of them are the armorial bearings of the family. Inside the fireplaces were installed 'two fine square steel stove grates, with globe heads, pedestal feet, obelisks and cut-work border', which were made by Thomas Chamberlain, ironmonger, at a cost of twenty-one pounds.

Benjamin Carter (who almost certainly did work in Northumberland House) and Sir Henry Cheere were other sculptors of note whose work is to be seen in some of the stately homes of today. The family of Carter had a sculptural business in Piccadilly and their work had wide-ranging influence. There are some very fine white marble chimneypieces by Thomas Carter in Blair Castle, Perthshire, where the size and splendour of the rooms make a fitting setting for them. The one in the drawing-room has delicately sculpted festoons and floral pendants with voluted jambs, like a spiral scroll, at sides and front. Above the mantel is set a picture by Zoffany, a conversation piece of the third Duke and Duchess of Atholl with their seven children. Corinthian columns on each side support a cornice and broken pediment containing an urn with trailing flowers.

Most of the chimneypieces in similar style have mirrors above them, but that in the dining-room at Blair Castle has an overmantel in the form of a trophy of arms of all periods. This was by the stuccoist

Thomas Clayton, the best known of the eighteenth-century workers in Scotland, but the marble mantelpiece with a head of Apollo on the frieze was made by Thomas Carter in 1751. It is a striking feature in a room of baroque grandeur.

It is because of this individual craftsmanship that the chimneypieces in the great houses are so peculiarly expressive of their age. We see the wonderful zest of the Renaissance world in their lavish use of decoration and flamboyant indulgence in colour being muted to a more restrained consciousness of line and proportion when the professional architects came on the scene, mounting to an occasional over-exuberance when designers such as Thomas Chippendale took a hand.

Chippendale, best known for his furniture, did not design many chimneypieces (*The Gentleman and Cabinet Maker's Director* of 1762 published some of them), but those he did are unmistakable for their extravagant rococo carving in the style of Louis XIV, where there is no place for a straight line. The design is often asymmetric, with a profusion of delicately executed ornament in imitation of rock work, shells, foliage and scrolls massed together.

This exuberant rococo decoration is seen at its best at Ham House, Surrey, where the chimneypiece in the north drawing-room is flanked by twisted half-columns entwined with vines and adorned with cupids. The inset picture over the mantel is also surrounded by clambering cupids and is generally attributed to Francis Cleyn, a German artist who was appointed to the Mortlake tapestry works by James I. There is an interesting link-up here, for the decorations of the chimneypiece are copied direct from one of Raphael's cartoons which often served as a model for the Mortlake weavers, suggesting that Cleyn was responsible for designing them (page 76).

During the Regency period and the reign of George IV the enthusiasm for Greek culture, foreshadowed by the Adam brothers, was reflected in all branches of art, and designs for chimneypieces were elaborated and made even more elegant. Everywhere the Greek anthemion ornament was seen, related in form to the flower of the honeysuckle, together with the formal stylised acanthus leaf, scrolls, foliage and ribbons. Craftsmanship was at its peak for the machine had

22 Rococo chimneypiece at Ham House, Surrey, with silver firepan

not yet come to take the place of the sensitive hands of the artist-craftsman.

A visit from royalty has always inspired a display of magnificence. This is borne out in many of the splendid features in stately homes of this period. At Burghley House, Stamford, seat of the Marquess of Exeter, a suite known as the George rooms contains some unique silver fireplaces. Though the great house was built by the first Lord Burghley, Lord High Treasurer to Queen Elizabeth I, these state rooms, extending along the southern side of the house, were prepared for a proposed visit from George IV when he was Prince of Wales in 1789. They reflect all the magnificence of a luxury-loving age.

The first room has a fine white marble chimneypiece inlaid with scagliola, after an Adam design, whilst the grate, fender and fire-irons are of burnished steel ornamented with silver of the Charles II period.

The silver fittings of the fireplaces in the third and fourth George rooms are also Charles II, with the mantelpiece in the former installed in 1790, the work of Bossi. The Adam chimneypiece in the great drawing-room, or fourth George room, is of white marble inlaid with Scottish granite, ornamented in the centre with a medallion portraying 'Danae in the Golden Shower'.

The most splendid chimneypiece of all is in the second room, known as the state bedroom after it was used by Queen Victoria and Prince Albert during their visit to Burghley in 1844. The chimneypiece, of carved white statuary marble, was made in Rome under the supervision of Piranesi, and it bears a resemblance to the work of Robert Adam, who was his pupil for some time. The jambs are of porphyry and upon them are sculptured bearded heads supporting the mantel. In the centre of the carved frieze is a porphyry tablet in mezzo relievo, or half-relief, representing the sacrifice of a goat. The grate, fender and fire-irons are of burnished steel with solid silver furnishings which include the lions and wheat-sheaves incorporated in the Exeter coat of arms. These were made in London about 1800.

Most of the applied silver ornamentation is detachable for easy cleaning, and so carefully has it been preserved for nearly 200 years that it shines out as beautifully as it did for its illustrious royal visitors.

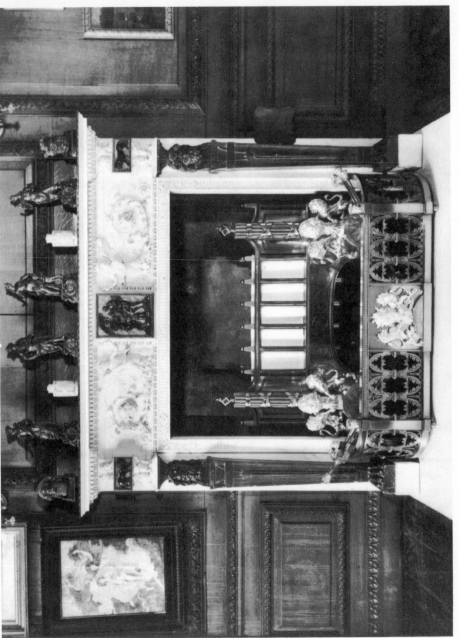

23 Silver-ornamented fireplace in the state bedroom at Burghley House

The 'Adam style' was adopted by people at all levels of society and the term has become synonymous with 'eighteenth-century' as a design label – although when a Gothic revival came toward the end of the eighteenth century, even Adam conformed when requested! A typical Gothic-revival fireplace shows ogee or S-shaped curves framing the fire opening and the overmantel, with indeterminate cusps, in the shape of small, roughly triangular projections, and a coved mantelshelf, the chimneypiece above it rising to the ceiling.

The elaborate type of decoration known as chinoiserie also became fashionable for a time. Sir William Chambers published a book of these designs after a visit to China, but not many of them survived. They were, perhaps, too bizarre for English tastes.

Some beautiful carved wood chimneypieces were produced towards the end of the eighteenth century by unknown craftsmen. In Ely House, Dover Street, London, once the town house of the Bishops of Ely, the carved pine fireplaces on the ground and first floors include the bishop's mitre in the exquisite carving – an example of the persistence of the practice of showing the owner's profession on the chimneypiece. The house was built 1772–6 by Sir Robert Taylor, architect to the Bank of England, and has been described as one of the finest surviving eighteenth-century mansions in London. It is now occupied by the Oxford University Press who allow the public free access during the day.

A carved pine chimneypiece in the Victoria & Albert Museum, reckoned to date from about the second quarter of the eighteenth century, is painted to look like stone. It has the ubiquitous caryatids with fruit baskets on their heads supporting the entablature, and a centre panel with a similar pleasing female face has a sunburst surround, with carved foliage on each side.

The next picture shows an original example of a carved wooden fireplace of the late eighteenth century, recently perfectly restored by Roger Board, an architectural woodcarver, and now in his home in Wimbledon. The chimneypiece, of pine, has enrichments carved in lime, pinned and glued to the main part after the manner of Grinling Gibbons. It has a flute and dart frieze with inset paterae in the centre, in the form of an ornament in low relief within a small round frame,

24 Restored fireplace of Adam design in a house at Wimbledon

while the moulding above it is in the formal acanthus-leaf pattern. The moulding round the fireplace opening has an egg and tongue pattern, and the corner blocks above the pilasters each side are enriched with the familiar honeysuckle, scroll and leaves. Some of the ribbons were badly broken when the chimneypiece came into Mr Board's possession but after his expert attention it is impossible to detect the old from the new. A Levanto marble surround and hearth set off a dog grate of the same period.

This was a period that saw some of the most elegant dog grates ever designed, the fronts generally in bright steel, with some parts of brass. They superseded the big cumbersome iron basket grates which had been designed to take logs or coal and had become uneconomical now that coal was in everyday use.

At this time John Adam joined the famous ironfounders, the Carron Company in Stirlingshire, in their early years. He was accepted as a partner in the company and the connection is still upheld today.

With his brothers Robert and James, John Adam created a new beauty in metal, gave it sweep and line, balance and proportion. Poised on slender pedestals the dog grates were polished till the iron seemed to turn to precious metal and they were called jewel dog grates. Adam designed, and the Carron foundrymen made, castings fretted and woven like black lace flowing into graceful curves.

From time to time the company reproduced a jewel dog grate of Adam design. The original is now on exhibition in an Adam chimney-piece in the Adam furniture section of the Victoria & Albert Museum. This grate was constructed with two fronts, a winter front for use when burning coal, and a summer front. They are beautifully fitted one over the other and fixed by a spring attachment, the summer front being easy to remove.

In the drawing-room at Osterley Park, Middlesex, Adam used 'paktong' for the dog grate, an alloy of zinc, copper and nickel which has a yellowish tinge. It was part of his experiments to bring all parts of a room into harmony with each other, but in general it was iron that was used, either cast in the furnaces of the great ironworks then spring-ing up, or wrought by the hands of a craftsman.

The hob grate also came into use during the last half of the eighteenth century, and designs for this kind of grate feature in some of the Adam drawings. The fronts were in cast iron, the bars, bowed or rounded, in wrought iron. The side panels were ornamented with great delicacy with an art that was never better understood than at this period. Again, the Carron Foundry in Scotland was responsible for a great many of these grates, particularly those ornamented in the formal style of the Adam brothers.

25 Late eighteenth-century double-ogee hob grate, after an Adam design, made by Carron

The Adam designs were modelled by William and Henry Haworth, who were students at the Royal Academy during the presidency of Sir Joshua Reynolds and were also pupils of the Adams. Their work was intricate and detailed, beautifully carved in wood before being fixed for ever in metal, in panels for grates, balconies and balustrades.

The three types of hob grate were the double semi-circle, the double ogee and rectangular cheeks. They were placed in a square recess surrounded by a frame of stone or marble. The recess above the hobs had a plastered back slanting up the chimney, and the sides were either plastered or lined with plates of fluted iron or Dutch tiles. There was no register door, but the short distance between the fire bars and the lintel prevented too much smoking.

Whilst architects were concentrating on the general design of fire-places, scientists were concerned with making the open fire more efficient, to use the radiant heat of the fuel economically and to give out less smoke. In the early part of the century, the 'ventilating' fireplace was invented by Nicolas Gauger, author of a treatise on *La Mecanique du Feu,* which was translated from the French and published in England by Dr Desaguliers. Gauger's fireplace had a curved back to reflect the rays of the fire into the room. At first it had a somewhat complicated arrangement of caliducts and it was difficult to clean and repair, so that it never really made its mark. Nevertheless, it was probably the fore-runner of many similar modern fireplaces so the idea was not totally lost.

The same may be said of the first smoke-consuming fireplaces, many of which were ingenious and complicated, never coming into general use because of their awkward appearance and the difficulties of managing them.

In the attempt to save the waste heat of the fuel by a reduction in the size of the chimney throat, a great deal is owed to Count Rumford, whose *Essays, Political, Economical, Philosophical* were published in 1798. Those who are interested in fireplace history would do well to read these essays and study the accompanying diagrams, for almost all grates of the succeeding century came to be based upon his theories. He aimed to improve the open fireplace by preventing that 'greatest of all plagues, a smoky chimney'. He deplored 'the enormous waste of fuel in London which may be estimated by the vast dark cloud which continually hangs over this great metropolis'.

Large fireplace openings were usual in his day and it was quite obvious that they needed to be lessened by building in the appropriate material. For this, Rumford recommended marble, fire-stone or bricks and mortar covered with a thin coating of plaster, whitewashed, as white reflects and radiates the heat as well as light. He would not advocate the use of metals, since they were conductors which would absorb the radiant heat from the fire and less would go into the room. The air coming into contact with metal would go up the chimney, and its use should be confined to the grate.

He considered register doors unnecessary, adding that it was merely necessary to remove local hindrances which prevent the smoke being forced up the chimney by the pressure of heavier air of the room. He seems to have been almost completely concerned with the proper formation of the mouth of the flue. Since his day, of course, there have been tremendous improvements in the type of grate used, in the amount of heat given out by the fuel, and in smoke abatement, aided by smokeless fuels.

Meanwhile, change was slow to come to the homes of the humble. In the cottage, country farmhouse or parsonage, the open fire was still used for cooking, with a great kettle suspended over it on an adjustable hanger to supply hot water. There was an ingenious device by which the kettle could be tipped to pour out the boiling water. A cauldron could be suspended in the same way to make the family porridge or some kind of stew.

Baking was done in a brick oven built by the side of the open fire so that the smoke from the oven could escape up the chimney. The oven was usually circular and domed over in brick, rather like the old Cornish cloam oven and worked on the same principle.

The new cooking ranges that came into being towards the end of the century were only an extension of this principle. In 1787 we read that Parson Woodforde had 'two stoves put in his kitchen', but we are not told whether they were the new kitchen ranges that had been patented by Thomas Robinson on 21 October 1780.

A description of one of these ranges runs thus:

One side of the fire is the oven and the other side is made to wind up with a cheeck. The top bar in front is made to fall down occasionally to a level with the second bar. The moving cheeck is made with a socket in it to receive a swinging trivet. The oven is made of cast iron, nearly square in front, the door hung with hinges and fastened with a handle and a turn-buckle and the oven is provided with fillets for the shelves to rest upon. The oven must be enclosed with bricks and mortar.

The old roasting ranges had cheeks that could be wound up to reduce the size of the fire. Robinson added the oven at the side, making it much more convenient for the smaller houses then being built in the suburbs of London and in big industrial towns.

So the last remnants of the old open fire, with all its cheerful, homely appurtenances, began to disappear, though slowly at first. A new era in the kitchen/living-room began. The kitchen range was here to stay and during the next century developed into an ingenious combination of cooker, heater and, eventually, hot-water supplier, but it needed far more attention and made more work in the form of black-leading, polishing and hearth cleaning than the old open fire ever demanded.

7

Victorian Battle of the Styles

The nineteenth century has gone down into history as the age of the Industrial Revolution, a time of change and turbulence, when England was a curious mixture of prosperity and poverty, virtue and vice, the latter carefully smothered under a heavy cloak of respectability. In a general sense it rejected the art of a previous age together with its extravagant, dissolute ways.

This changed outlook was reflected very clearly in the design of houses and their interiors which lost the grace and elegance of Regency days and became stolid and heavy-looking. Paradoxically, it was also the age of revivals of past styles of architecture. Tradition began to break up and a new freedom of thought prevailed. There were some personal innovations here and there, chosen chiefly for convenience or for the feelings they aroused.

Thus in the early part of the century Georgian art was in vogue, and this was followed by the Greek, Gothic and Elizabethan styles, used successively and indiscriminately, resulting in confused uncertainty and what has become known as the Battle of the Styles.

At their worst, early nineteenth-century fireplaces consisted of slabs of marble put together for jambs and lintel, with another slab for the shelf. Occasionally some mouldings relieved the otherwise bare surface.

At its best, the Greek revival period showed a kind of austere classicism that was at least restful to the eye. A white marble pediment would be above the frieze, with acroteria, pedestals for the support of statues or carved ornaments, at the corners. A series of small paterae ornamented the frieze, and the fireplace opening was framed by a semicircular arch, simply moulded, to set off a polished steel grate.

Gone were the days when sculptor and artist transformed the chimneypiece into a centre of applied art. Instead there was an overmantel of looking-glass over a simple marble chimneypiece. Sometimes there would be some Greek ornamentation or sphinx heads on the pilasters of the overmantel, for the sphinx became a popular decorative feature after Napoleon's campaign in Egypt.

Sir John Soane, the famous nineteenth-century architect, brought a new treatment to bear on chimneypieces by placing the frieze immediately below the entablature and over the opening mould, in line with the caps of the pilasters, thus giving them greater length without raising the height of the shelf. It was still fashionable to keep mantels low so that people could see their reflections with ease. A marble chimneypiece of this design is to be seen in Sir John Soane's house (now an architectural museum) in Lincoln's Inn Fields, London. It is particularly interesting because it shows the contemporary fire grate, fire irons and fender.

The early Victorian period brought a return of romanticism which expressed itself in neo-Gothic and Elizabethan styles, often in regrettable taste. The arbiter of taste now became the middle class – the rising industrialist, as opposed to the Regency aristocrat, and in general fireplace design, along with interior decoration as a whole, abandoned all ideas of Georgian harmony. Poor imitation was encouraged by a less discriminating clientele, and strange mixtures of all kinds of ornament resulted, so that medieval, Renaissance and naturalistic motifs were seen in superfluous association on all kinds of things.

There were, however, some notable exceptions, which, if they did not prove the rule, proved that some Victorians knew how to create an atmosphere of stately grandeur that was comparable with any other period. One of the famous mansions of this time (now open to the public at stated times) is Lancaster House, London, and the fireplaces in the state rooms are both interesting and beautiful with a distinctive character of their own. The house was built for the Duke of Sutherland by Benjamin Wyatt early in the last century and is preserved much as it was in its Victorian heyday. The interior is very noticeably under the French influence which was just then beginning to pervade English interior decoration. In fact it bears a marked resemblance to the splendours of Versailles, with chimneypieces and looking-glass over-mantels after the French style.

The Garibaldi room, which commemorates a visit of the Italian patriot, has an original grey marble mantelpiece with a huge cockleshell design in the centre of the frieze and heavy carved voluted jambs. A fine Italian gilt-framed mirror hangs over it. In the west drawing-room (formerly the Duchess' boudoir) is a remarkable chimneypiece in white marble with the figures of Summer and Winter on the jambs in bold relief. A swan with outspread wings over swags of foliage covers the frieze, and over it all is a tall gilt-framed mirror with the Duke of Sutherland's monogram above it, the delicately wrought French work in direct contrast to the boldness of the marble chimneypiece beneath.

In the state drawing-room small gilded caryatids support the marble mantelshelf, elaborately enriched, the fireplaces having their original kerbs; but the most resplendent of the chimneypieces adorns the great gallery, an apartment over 120ft in length. The inner wall of the middle section is designed with three tall round-headed recesses, the middle one containing the chased and gilded chimneypiece of veined marble with ormolu enrichments. Its shelf is supported by allegorical figures representing Architecture and Painting. Above the fire opening is the Sutherland monogram flanked by cherubs and in each spandrel a ducal coronet.

It is an awe-inspiring composition, worthy of the distinguished assemblies of the élite of Victorian London that once gathered here. In fact, Lancaster House was bought and given to the nation by the first Viscount Leverhulme, and now comes under the jurisdiction of the Department of the Environment: it is now used as a centre of government hospitality, so the state rooms not infrequently see assemblies equal in importance to any that have gone before. The house is open to the public at most weekends.

26 Elaborate chased and gilded chimneypiece in the Great Gallery, Lancaster House, London

Another of the finest surviving examples of Victorian interior decor-ation may be seen at Knebworth House, Hertfordshire, in the state drawing-room. When the novelist Bulwer-Lytton inherited the place in 1843 it was the time of the revival of interest in High Gothic and his aim was to turn it into a Gothic palace. He had architects at work during much of his tenancy. John Crace of Wigmore Street, the artist and designer and author of *The Art of Colour Decoration*, redesigned the state drawing-room with Bulwer-Lytton. Some of the most elaborate high-Victorian decoration is seen in the chimneypiece which has an overmantel mirror framed with niches containing figures, and pinnacles coloured and gilded soaring almost to ceiling height and terminating in two red-gowned angels supporting a shield.

The carved stonework and the arched fire opening, with the spandrel space included in the panel of crests, has a splendid marble bittern in the centre, complementing those on the tall wrought-iron fire-dogs. The bittern is a bird which appears in the Lytton family crest and is seen again and again at Knebworth. It is repeated in the tiles of the deep reveals each side of the wide fireplace, which has a wrought-iron fire-basket and fender. The tiles were specially made for this fireplace, for each one bears a motto or a crest of the Bulwer-Lytton families. There is also a family motto inscribed on the coving below the mantel-shelf.

On a less grandiose scale is the fireplace in Mrs Bulwer-Lytton's bedroom. It is of two-toned marble flanked by round classical columns, with a wood overpiece painted white and a ribbon festoon-type decor-ation picked out in gold. Above the mantelshelf is a panel bearing the inscription 'This room long occupied by Elizabeth Bulwer-Lytton and containing the relics most associated with her memory. Her son trusts that her descendants will preserve unaltered – Liberis Virtutis Exemplar'.

A black iron sarcophagus-type grate fills the fire opening. It has spikes above the fire bars to keep the fuel from rolling out. A black curved fender on small feet stands well within the hearth. With the other fireplaces in the house this one points the differences of style at this time.

In the smaller Victorian house, overmantel mirrors were much in vogue. Often they were framed in pinewood and painted or gilded, with ornament of composition, and they were frequently of a bold design that tended to be overpowering in a small room.

As Victoria's reign wore on the design of fireplaces became even more varied. The rediscovery of the Tudor tradition around 1870 resulted in a burst of pseudo-Tudor architecture, twisted chimneys and huge stone fireplaces becoming fashionable. It also brought back a semblance of the great oak chimneypieces of that period, but with Victorian innov-

27 Victorian fireplace in embossed ceramic tiles, made in 1870 by Maw & Co

ations. A wide mantelshelf supported on brackets immediately above the fireplace opening carried a series of thin turned balusters and little balustrades dividing the shelf into compartments designed to hold the innumerable knickknacks so beloved of the Victorians.

In the smaller houses and villas then springing up in the towns and cities, the fireplaces, diminished in size, were finished by a simple slate surround with a plain mantelshelf, on which stood the prefabricated wooden overmantel bought from the furnishers, lavishly adorned with little shelves, small twiddly balusters and mirrors.

There are few, if any, genuine Victorian fireplaces left in ordinary homes. They have all been pulled out long ago and replaced by modern appliances. We have to rely on old prints and photographs to see what they looked like in their original setting.

It was not unusual to see a parlour crammed with cumbersome furniture, all heavily draped, for the Victorians had a passion for covering everything up, as if the naked article offended their sense of propriety. The mantelshelf, of wood or cast iron, would be covered with a mantel board made of thick serge material or velvet, with ball fringe round the edge, designed to catch the maximum amount of dust. These, and the display of small ornaments on the overmantel, must have been the despair of many an overworked housemaid.

Nevertheless, this was a miscellaneous age of conflicting moods, when the Industrial Revolution brought a great many things within the reach of ordinary people. There were, for instance, some beautiful ceramic tiles made at this time, and like much other Victoriana they have now become collector's pieces, much sought after. Cast-iron interiors and tiled reveals are characteristic features of the age. There were also some fully tiled fireplaces which showed Victorian ceramic art at its best. There is another unusual fireplace in the offices of the Fulham Pottery, London, where it is believed to have been made. It is basically of glazed stone, richly decorated. The pattern was incised while the clay was still soft, then painted cobalt blue. Two niches in the jambs hold large stone figures of a traditional woodcutter with a load of logs on his back. There is a kerb decorated with cobalt and the whole gives an interesting sidelight on the potter's art at that time.

Early in the nineteenth century fire openings became completely filled in with black iron, and the arched opening displaying the grate was also of iron. It seems that Count Rumford's carefully propounded theories did not make any lasting impression on anyone, since these cast-iron interior grates became standard. In the best houses the fire basket was surrounded by ground and polished steel plates framed with brass mouldings, but there was a gradual diminution in the size of the chimney. A flue of about 14 × 9 inches or even less was considered sufficient to take away the smoke, and the average fire area was not much more. In order to take the flue it was necessary to make the wall thicker, and the fire was projected forward into the room as a chimney

28 Cast bronze and brass closed stove designed by Alfred Stevens, c1851

breast. The chimneypiece was made more important where it covered the whole of this projection, and it would also add to the efficiency of the fire. The fire was found to burn more economically when a register door to the grate was provided, the opening to be adjusted to regulate the passage of air through it.

These grates were often quite decorative, with engraved fronts in polished steel, and pierced and engraved aprons and fenders to a similar design.

A movable grate was shown at the Universal Exhibition of 1855, where the fuel rested on a small carriage fitted with wheels or castors so that it could be brought forward into the room when the fire was alight and burning well. The smoke passed into a chimney through a flue made of sliding tubes fitting into each other rather like those of a telescope. In theory it was feasible, but it cannot have worked well in practice, for it never became popular.

Many different arrangements giving a reversed draught effect were tried, but all were liable to smoke and clog with soot.

Closed stoves never really played much part in the English home, though there were some attractive ones made at this time. A particularly good one was designed by Alfred Stevens and made by Hoole & Co in 1851. It was in cast bronze and brass with panels of moulded earthenware (page 93). A free-standing heating stove was made in Germany about 1880, but few of them were used here.

When anthracite began to be used as a fuel, closed stoves found a place in a hall or other rooms where slow combustion was desirable. They were used in living rooms far more widely on the Continent, where they became a well-known decorative feature.

In the kitchen, progress was being made with the open range developed by Robinson. It had adjustable bars to reduce the size of the fire, a trivet to take the kettle and a boiler which had to be filled by hand.

The Bodley Range, patented in 1802, demonstrated that heat could be conducted in horizontal flues if there was a sufficiently high vertical chimney to create a draught. This was said to be the first kitchen range with a closed top and the fire open in front, and all kitcheners from that time appear to have descended from it.

To keep its fire box full up, so that the top could be used for boiling and the oven for roasting, meant a fuel consumption of some twelve to fifteen scuttles of coal a day. No doubt these Bodley Ranges cooked the food adequately and made kitchens cosy, but they poured out the thick smoke that so often made nineteenth-century London fog-bound and produced the dreaded choking 'pea-souper' that killed people in thousands.

Speaking generally, in the average middle-class Victorian home the fireplace was just what it should be – solid, respectable (no caryatids here!), with no rococo frivolity. The general rule was for a heavy white marble mantelshelf supported on corbels for the drawing-room, with a similar one in black marble for the dining-room, perhaps with some inlaid panels of coloured marbles in the wide jambs.

In the small servantless home the kitchen, with its open range, continued to be the living-room for the family, the parlour, stuffed with the household treasures, being strictly reserved for use on high days and holidays (Plate 30).

As through all the foregoing periods, the fireplace was a faithful reflection of a way of life, the family meeting place. It was also a true indication of social progress, yet parts of the north of England and the Highlands of Scotland were just about giving up the central hearth in favour of a gable and fireplace, with a wide timber hood over it to channel the smoke upwards. The open hearth was still big enough for peats to be tumbled on to it, and the homely black kettle and the iron cooking-pot were always in evidence.

8

The Gradual Decline of the Open Fire

By the beginning of the twentieth century the Englishman's home had, by various stages of development, attained a degree of comfort unrivalled anywhere in the world. Adequate heating was high on the list of his priorities and fireplaces were automatically installed in every room in the house, excepting only the meanest of attics.

By about 1900, neo-Gothic architecture had gone out of fashion and the emphasis had shifted to sham Tudor, with as much timbering as possible. Architectural plans of that period suggest that style was subjugated to the convenience and completeness of the domestic apartments, but the designs were not usually unpleasing. There were in fact a medley of designs, that could well have in them a little of all periods if they fitted a client's requirements. This applied to fireplaces as much as anything, since they were the first consideration in any house.

In Victorian days the open brick fireplace was seldom seen. It was almost regarded as a novelty. Now, with the Art Nouveau style gaining ground among the Edwardians, the inglenook was revived, with a great deal more to it than the Tudors ever dreamed of.

None of the country houses being built at this time was complete without at least one or two of these elaborate fireplaces. A design for an eight-bedroom house at Potter's Bar, Hertfordshire, in 1910 shows an inglenook in the dining-room which appears to be a small room in itself. The grate is surrounded by a plain beaten-copper frame and hood; on either side, recesses are formed in the wall for a tobacco jar, or the like, and above are a series of small cupboards and openings for the display of china. The nook is lined with red bricks and has plain low oak settles on either side with a side window for reading, so that the whole forms a comfortable lounge, completely draughtproof.

Sometimes a more formal treatment was given by using tiled surrounds and an overmantel, still using the space above for small cupboards. The overmantel was usually carried up to the picture rail, with small windows on either side. Either way it was a composition that emphasised the importance of the fireplace.

The hall – or sitting-hall as it was called, because of its size – was usually provided with a fireplace that was singled out for architectural treatment, and one design of that period shows a graceful dog grate surrounded by a treatment of Ionic pilasters and entablature, and provided with a sitting or club fender, a very comfortable feature in a hall.

In general, fireplaces were given character by including the whole of the chimney breast in the design and the materials chosen for them were selected to harmonise with the rooms, each of which was used for a definite purpose and furnished to that end.

A grate with tiled sides and a Portland stone architrave would probably have a huge chimneypiece flanked by Ionic pilasters of oak. This was considered suitable for a library.

A country-house drawing-room was treated in a lighter key. Most probably had cream-enamelled panelling on the walls, and the fireplace, designed to include the whole of the chimney breast, would have a pine mantel enamelled white, with small columns and recesses for ornaments. A grate of polished steel with wide splays of old green tiles enclosed in an architrave of green Connemara marble completed the typical fireplace of its time.

In a country-house dining-room an overmantel might have panels into which various coloured woods were introduced to form a geometrical pattern, and this would look perfect in its setting.

A simple roundel set in an oak mantel was a design favoured by Sir

Edward Lutyens. It was an effective means of commemorating a person or even an incident. We see it in the library at Knebworth House, where Lutyens removed John Crace's elaborate Victorian decorations and substituted a plain oak chimneypiece with a marble bolection moulding framing the fire opening. The marble roundel portrays Robert, first Earl of Lytton in his later years, and was made by Sir Alfred Gilbert as a model for his memorial in St Paul's Cathedral.

Rather more formal were the late Renaissance revivals that found their way into many graceful Edwardian drawing-rooms, the over-mantel being designed as a frame for a picture and the whole enclosed in an architectural setting.

The woodcarver's art lived on in post-Renaissance fashion, and now and again one comes across examples of carved wooden mantels that were made in the first part of this century. There is one at Burghley House in the pagoda room which has a little history attached to it: it was carved by Belgian refugees during World War I from chestnut grown in Burghley Park. The subject of the carving along the frieze is a battle scene from one of the great battles of the time and, appropriately, the heads of Earl Kitchener and Sir John French are at each end.

It is indeed a permanent reminder of a period of history that had shattering effects on the great landowners, for the era of the stately home – at least as a purely private residence – was drawing to an end.

Whilst the general design of fireplaces represented some facets of every period, the design of grates was moving forwards. There were many kinds available at this period. Those designed by Dr T. Pridgin-Teale represented the scientific application of sound principles to the domestic hearth, and slow-combustion stoves after his model were a great improvement on previous kinds where about five-sixths of the heat went up the flue. The basis of his improvements, soon to be followed by others, was the use of firebrick sides and back, and small front and bottom iron bars. These kept the coal in position without hindering combustion. In one model the back was inclined forward to increase the intensity of the heat and to diffuse it more widely by throwing it forward into the room.

In some designs a movable ashpan regulated the draught and helped combustion as well as aiding the removal of ashes. A supply of fresh warmed air was obtained by means of an inlet flue, fed by external air which was heated by the fire.

There was also a well fire, where the coals were placed upon a back perforated hearth which had underneath it a small chamber lined with fireclay in which air was heated to a high temperature before passing

29 Tiled register grate with barless fire (Lee & Girvan)

through the fire. Air was often supplied to the fire by ducts contained in the depths of the front hearth.

Another kind of grate was known as a tilt fire; it was tilted upwards, with the bottom bars in an almost vertical position, and would burn for some hours without attention. It was not unlike a dog grate in appearance and could be removed in summer to make way for flowers or shrubs.

Another of the dog-grate type, known as the Nautilus stove, was also free-standing – and provided with wheels so that it could be moved easily – and its heat radiated from all sides. The flue opening at the back was much smaller than that of ordinary stoves. This stove was also used in conjunction with a suitable boiler and pipes to heat two or three small radiators in the house.

Sometimes a fire was made direct upon the ordinary hearth without using any grate at all, but this method was not very economical, nor did it give any more heat.

Between the wars, barless fires with deep bottom grates on feet replaced the bar-fronted grates and many people had new fronts fitted to the old grates. It was possible to hook boiling trivets on to these fronts and to use fire tables around them, curved and made to fit the grate. They were finished in stove-enamelled black, chromium-plate, brass or copper and stainless steel. These grates on the whole were adaptable and made a cheerful fire. The one drawback was the dreary surround that came into fashion at the same time.

The all-tile 'arch' grate went into the 1930s, when the fully tiled fireplace arrived as cement fondu was invented and took the place of Portland cement. Plain beige slabbed tiles with a slabbed raised hearth or kerb were a travesty of the elegant styles of earlier years. Sometimes a lustre strip was allowed to relieve the monotony but it did little to enhance the general appearance. One wonders what happened to all the beautiful Victorian tiles and Dutch tiles that were so ruthlessly discarded at that time.

This was a period when interior decoration reached its lowest ebb. The fashion for the all-beige room, devoid of ornaments and pictures made the interior stark and featureless.

In fact, we were getting so near to ruling out all that was decorative that the so-called art that was left was becoming almost indistinguishable from utility. It reduced the fireplace to a dull, unimaginative nonentity which succeeding generations naturally had no compunction in discarding.

Nevertheless, the 1930s did eventually show a resurgence of feeling against the 'clinical look', and a 're-creation' in decorative art began to show itself, as colour and various kinds of ornamentation came back. The prevailing need for economy kept the question of simplicity before them, but it is significant that designers again began to link the fireplace with décor, though with caution at first.

A design book of 1932 shows a return to the use of marble, and a London house is depicted with a mantelpiece and kerb of black marble, the inside of the fireplace being of polished firebrick. Tall triple mirrors formed a kind of overmantel, with edgings shaded from dark to light grey and a band around the central mirror in iridescent red glass. It was elegantly austere, and marked a welcome drift away from the tasteless beige tiles. Other designers began to follow suit, and in the years immediately following we see living-room interiors with fire-places in travertine marble, polished Portland stone, Ancaster stone and similar materials.

Various materials were also used together. In the dining-room of a house in Lancashire the fireplace was of Hopton Wood stone with a stainless-steel surround and a walnut mantelpiece. This admixture of materials set the trend for fireplaces for some years to come. Though none of the designs had the importance of a Renaissance chimneypiece or the eye-catching qualities of a modern fireplace, at least they were coming back to something that was decorative as well as functional.

Around 1937 a new Esse heating stove made its appearance. It could be set in a surround and hearth to match the general décor of a room. It was quite pleasing to look at and was a very efficient room heater.

The year 1935 marked the invention of the now famous Baxi Patent Fire, with controlled underfloor draught. The idea originated from Mr John Baxendale, the present chairman of the family firm of iron-founders in Lancashire. Compelled to clean out his own fireplace for a short time, he began to think in terms of a simpler kind of grate, one that would be easy to clean and easy to light and maintain. After many experiments he finally perfected a fire with controlled draught piped to the ash-pit, and a high capacity, easily removable ash-box. Unlike other fires, which need to take air or draught from the room in which they are installed, the Baxi takes its combustion air from underneath the floor space or from outside the house, the amount admitted being controlled by a lever. This results in a greater volume of air being pulled through the fire-bed and a more reactive burning.

So the Baxendale invention united the traditional appeal of the open fire with modern standards of convenience and cleanliness. Production and marketing of this new fireplace had barely started when the war came and the Baxi Foundry switched to day and night munitions work. Nevertheless, the pattern of post-war development had been set; heating appliances would be designed to give the maximum comfort with the minimum work.

Today this kind of fire is installed in well over half a million homes in England alone, in a great variety of settings, both classical and modern. It has gone a long way to returning to favour the cheerful, open fire, for its perfect control means that a bright blaze can be obtained in a moment and it need never go out.

To a large extent these fires at floor level took the place of the ubiquitous all-night burner that was designed to burn anything combustible during the lean war years and immediately afterwards. They stood fairly high on the hearth and had a deep space beneath them for the ashes, which still had to be cleaned out frequently although the fire kept in well.

With the advent of smokeless fuel and the gradual enforcement in big cities of the Clean Air Act the popularity of these fires began to wane. Gas or electrical appliances were flooding into the market, and before very long central heating began to be within the reach of most middle-class homes.

In the kitchen, the turn of the century saw great changes. A new type of range, known as the Swinton (patented by Barraclough), combined an open fire with a cooking range.

It was made to fit into the fireplace and had a simple lifting rack so that the bottom grate could be raised to reduce the size of the fire. It had a boiler attached and it also had bottom heat to the oven, roasting bars so that roasting could be done in front of the fire and an iron bracket rest. It could be used either as a closed or open fire, regulated by a butterfly damper or a pull-out damper, according to choice, and there was an ash-pan and cinder sifter to ease the domestic chores.

The manufacturers claimed that this range saved over 50 per cent in fuel. To add to its attractions there was a range of decorative tiles from which the customer could choose for covings, jamb mouldings and hearth. They were in different colours and designs and made a colourful finish to the assembly. Sometimes a cast-iron mantelpiece was added which could be painted to match the tiles.

There is no doubt that it was an efficient and popular design and soon

30 Mid-Victorian kitchener in a cottage at Selsted, Kent. It is set between two brick hobs

found favour with the new house builders. At that time there were hundreds of foundries in the north of England working to produce different types of cooking ranges. William Barraclough of Pudsey, Yorkshire, was one of the largest manufacturers, with teams of horses and carts delivering their fireplaces all over the county. Their former grazing grounds are now a trading estate, which gives an idea of the number of horses they kept. They specialised in the supply of bottom grates of various shapes and sizes and even now have over 400 different kinds in the pattern room. Unfortunately, the bulk of old patterns for ranges have been destroyed, but the old catalogues that remain give a fairly accurate idea of what they looked like and how they worked.

The first rival to the open fire for cooking was gas, and around 1907 some combination coal and gas cooking ranges appeared on the market, having a gas oven lined with enamelled plates and a gas hob with reversible gas grilling-burners and boiling-ring.

From this time onwards the cooking range was doomed in all but those areas where gas was not yet available. Hundreds of fine old ranges, with their polished steel and brass fittings and old tiles, were torn out and their places taken by the anonymous-looking domestic boiler for heating water and a gas stove for cooking.

There was however a compromise in a new type of range/fireplace, designed to satisfy all the usual family heating, cooking and hot water requirements in one compact unit. Its finish in vitreous enamel, easy to clean, appealed to the housewife who was weary of blackleading and polishing. It had a side oven, a boiler and an overnight burning fire, with a hinged closed fire-lid forming an additional hot plate. It became very popular in small homes for its economy and adaptability, but generally speaking, between the wars, the old-fashioned range began to disappear. The side pan had given way to a back boiler with pipes connecting it to the kitchen sink and the bathroom. Everyone was clamouring for labour-saving apparatus and naturally enough, the first impact was felt in the kitchen.

The pattern of society was changing radically. The big house owners, no longer so fabulously wealthy, found themselves with few servants left to stoke the fires and had to seek other means of heating their great cold rooms. The ordinary folk, enjoying a taste of freedom from slavery in other people's houses, were disinclined to make labour in their own homes. The answer came in central heating – or the gas or electric fire – and the open fire was abolished in all but the living-room in most homes.

9

The Development of Chimneys

The use of chimneys is first recorded in the year 1200, and these were additions for kitchens only. The flue leading to a chimney as we now understand it developed during the Norman period of architecture, the principle being comparable to that followed today.

In Chapter 2 we saw how a channel or funnel over a fireplace was used to carry off smoke. Medieval chimneys were made of wattle or clay, or lath and plaster, supported on a timber frame; the clay got slowly baked and became as hard as stone. The part which projected above the roof was constructed in a similar way and kept in repair by frequent coats of limewash. Later, a smoke chamber, like a small room, was formed above the fireplace and supported on the wide mantelbeam. According to various ordinances, some dating from the early fifteenth century, the construction of these wooden chimneys was prohibited in towns because of fire risk, but the practice continued in remote parts for many years.

In stone buildings, such as castles, the chimneys were also of stone, the earliest types being in the form of a shaft on an outside wall with side vents through which the smoke escaped just below the pointed top. A thirteenth-century Gothic type, usually built of rubble masonry, had lancet-shaped smoke outlets in the gablets. By the middle Gothic period these chimneys became very varied in design, with short shafts, octangular or square, finished with a battlemented cornice that looked imposing against the sky.

31 (a) fifteenth-century stone chimney; (b) Tudor brick chimneys; (c) seventeenth-century stone chimney

The fourteenth and the early fifteenth century were known as the
Decorated Period with good reason, for the masons extravagantly
lavished their skill on their stonework wherever they could, knobs and
bosses, naturalistic foliage and faces – grotesque or cherubic – cropping
up wherever possible, and some very beautiful and unusual turret
chimneys appeared. Judging by contemporary drawings, some of them
appeared to have been inspired by the old smoke louvres. With a battlemented and moulded cap, they added a final touch of richness to any
building.

For some time chimneys were an addition to a building, rather than
an integral part of it. As fireplace recesses were deepened and walls

built not so thick, the chimney had to project either on the outside or the inside of the wall, the external type being the earlier. Later, when chimneys became part of the general design of a house, they were sometimes grouped.

The chimney stack as such owes its origin to the use of coal. Henry III granted the people of Newcastle-on-Tyne a charter to dig for coal in 1239 and in Scotland the Abbot of Dunfermline was granted a charter in 1291, but it was mostly used in industry, and there was much prejudice against it. The first recorded use in London is in 1280, but by 1306 it was prohibited by proclamation, banned as a public nuisance because it was thought to corrupt the air.

Wood was the fuel in ordinary use, but towards the end of Elizabeth's reign it was becoming scarce, and there was a great outcry against its waste. The country's timber was being burnt up on open fires at an alarming rate and there was a scarcity for use in carpentry. This was when coal came into general domestic use, a regular trade in it beginning about 1561. According to Stow, noblemen who had town houses within the gates of London were being driven by 'the horrid fumes' from the increasing number of coal fires to migrate westwards into the prevailing wind, to build new mansions on the bank of the river towards Westminster. To distinguish the new fuel from the old coal – now called charcoal – it was known as sea-coal because it was brought to London and the east-coast towns by boat from the Northumberland coalfield.

Though it had to be used, it was not popular in all quarters. In *The English Fireplace,* Shuffrey tells us that the 'fair sex were most hostile to its use, as it was thought to give the coal tinge to the complexion, and it was considered a mark of respect when entertaining guests to warm the room with charcoal.' The smoke from coal was indeed intolerable and the chimney stack became a necessity to take the fumes right away from the house.

Originally each flue had a separate 'stalk' or stack, with its own cap and base, the grouping of flues into one large stack coming in late Tudor times. The chimney shafts were at first attached to each other in a solid block until it was found better to separate them, attaching them to each other at cap and base only. This let the wind through freely, thus getting rid of the down-draught caused by the wind hitting a solid block of masonry and blowing down the chimney opening.

The idea of building a storeyed wing with four flues in one stack probably originated in mid-Tudor times. One has only to study an old print of London at this time to see a veritable forest of chimneys projected against the sky. Almost every room now had its fireplace in the wall, and the outside of the house appeared to be covered with tall chimney stacks. Even so, it took more than a century for the same idea to spread to remote districts in Wales.

Tudor chimney stacks were nothing if not elaborate. It was primarily the use of brick that gave them their characteristic appearance. The bricklayer was a new craftsman, as eager to exercise his skill as were the stone masons and wood carvers, and he made his chimneys to appeal to the eye as well as to the practical senses. Medieval bricks were burnt with wood fuel in a clamp or kiln, and being insufficiently burnt they came out a beautiful warm crimson colour. The craftsmen who came from the Low Countries introduced endless ways of moulding and shaping the clay before firing it to the form desired. They also used an axe for the fine scorings with which they decorated it and a float stone for smoothing it. The sixteenth-century brickmakers produced some of the most beautiful and distinctive chimneys of any age.

In the south and east of England, where brick was used extensively, there was a craze for fancy shapes. The tall twisted chimneys of the manor house became a familiar part of its design; in fact the zig-zags and the spirals may well have been intended to draw attention to the number of chimneys, a status symbol, for by this time every room of importance was expected to have a fireplace. It was not unknown for people to erect a sham chimney to deceive the neighbours (just as in the 1950s people put up a television aerial with the same purpose in mind).

The great chimney stacks of the Tudor kitchens of Hampton Court Palace, with their beautifully moulded brick chimneys, are a fine example of their kind. Though scarcely one is original they are such faithful copies of the fantastic designs of the sixteenth-century brick-layer that they may be said to represent his work.

The yeoman farmer soon took up this idea of having decorative chimneys, and his farmhouse displayed a massive stack in the form of a cluster of chimneys, often beautifully ornamented. Each chimney might have a different pattern, set diagonally or square and completed with rich mouldings, but the favourite was still the spiral. It is still possible to see in a village street the original great solid chimney stack in a farmhouse, now probably subdivided into cottages, with smaller stacks around it.

At Steventon, Berkshire, an old house in The Causeway has one of these clusters in brick, all of different designs, with a huge chimney breast to the street, an obvious later addition to the medieval house. There is another cluster on a row of small houses in Albury, Surrey, though here their height tends to be overpowering.

The convenience and economy of a chimney stack in the centre of a house were obvious. It gave direct heat to two rooms, with the two fireplaces backing on to each other, and convected heat to the two rooms immediately above them.

William Harrison, an Essex clergyman, writing his *Description of England* (1577), said old men in his village 'have noted three things to be marvellously altered in England'. Among these were 'the multitude of chimneys lately erected'. Harrison deplored the passing of the central hearth; he saw it as a softening of men's characters 'from oke to willow'. As the smoke was supposed to harden the timbers of a house, so it was supposed to harden the human constitution. But neither Harrison nor his followers could stop progress, and as the end of the Tudor period overlapped the beginning of the Renaissance movement in England there was great striving toward better things and more comfort, for people of all classes.

Designs in brick became less fanciful and more uniform during the last half of the sixteenth century. The chimney stack lost some of its ornate late-Tudor carving. Nevertheless, in general it remained a massive structure, either rectangular or cruciform or simply circular, with a cap in the form of a classical order with projecting courses of bricks, sometimes with star-shaped tops. In East Anglia the builders showed a preference for diagonal chimneys, sometimes varied by a peculiar zig-zag form.

There was also a change, and greater variety of design, in stone chimneys. Burghley House, Stamford, is one of the earliest important Renaissance buildings erected in England by foreigners, and the great Barnack ragstone chimney shafts are in the form of Doric columns, with cap, base and entablature complete. Sometime in the nineteenth century they were castellated in neo-Gothic style, so that each one appears to have a small castle on its summit. A great range of these chimneys is seen on the north front of the house, outlined against the sky in massive dignity.

In the oolite stone district, of which the Cotswolds form an important section, the chimneys are a pleasing feature, nearly all constructed with rectangular shafts for each flue, formed of thin slabs of ashlar capped in the simplest fashion with a mould. The Gothic section is frequently seen to be retained in the base.

A seventeenth-century Cotswold cottage, solidly built in local limestone, usually had a distinctive style of its own, with a roof ridge nearly as high as the building itself. A tall stone chimney stack with a bold cornice was one of its main characteristic features.

A cottage or farmhouse chimney was sometimes given importance by means of stepped gablets or crow steps at the base, following roughly the slope of the roof behind. This design is most noticeable in areas where the Flemings settled.

The bigger cottages were often built in the same general shape as farmhouses – single-span with a central chimney stack, but the stack was rarely quite in the middle. It would be built first of all, and would steady the whole structure of the house, particularly where it served as a support for the staircase. The kitchen always had to be bigger than the parlour, and with the stack inside the building the outside appearance became decidedly one-sided – a fact which seems to have troubled no one!

The small cottages never aspired to moulded brickwork and decoration, except perhaps for some plain projecting courses, but they always managed to look charming and original. Many country cottages of the sixteenth and seventeenth century have big outside chimney stacks. In parts of the West Midlands it is quite common to see a little 'black and white' cottage with a rather cumbersome masonry chimney stack built on to the gable-end, probably as an afterthought. Some also have a brick oven built on to the base under a lean-to roof. Where there was a separate kitchen and parlour, each had its own chimney stack rising from the ends of the building, though this must have meant a great loss of heat.

Imposing though some of the chimney stacks were, they were far from efficient. The first recorded effort to study the smoking chimney was made about this time, during the first half of the seventeenth century. Louis Savot, a physician of Paris, made a study of architecture from the sanitary angle, but his theories were only partly successful. His idea was to lessen the width of the fireplace opening, so that less cold air could enter on each side of the fire. He also demonstrated that the flue should be smooth to minimise the friction of the ascending smoke and so save heat. Other ideas soon followed, all based on improving the chimney draught, but most of these early attempts were made at the expense of ventilating the room and were not wholly successful.

Though coal or wood were the fuels most generally used, turf and peat were the staple fuels in the North, particularly in the dales of Yorkshire, until well on into the eighteenth century. Many of the tracks leading down from the Yorkshire moors at the present time are in fact the old 'turf roads' down which the loads of fuel were brought on wooden sledges hauled by horses. In Devon and Cornwall, or the south-west region, where timber was scarce, peat and furze were the most common fuels, stacked ready for use in the 'ookener' on the right-hand side of the fireplace.

Since coal is slower burning than wood or peat it became possible to use smaller grates, specially designed to take it. They were usually free-standing, basket-shaped and raised upon four legs. This meant that chimney breasts could be made narrower and the width of the chimney openings restricted, so that in many cases a man could no longer climb up to clean them; for the next two or more centuries the chimney sweeping was done exclusively by boys – as any reader of *The Water Babies* will know.

During the last half of the seventeenth century chimneys became more formal in design, the aim being to give a symmetrical effect when seen from the front of a building. They lost their elaborate Jacobean shafting and became a huge square or cruciform structure, with the flues concealed inside. In general, a plain rectangular stack, with moulded plinth and cornice, is seen on Wren's buildings. Those on Chelsea Royal Military Hospital, London, are a typical example of his passion for symmetry. This general plan set the pattern for most of the following century. The chimney stack merged into the design rather than being an important part in its own right, and so lost its character.

Cottages were not affected by this new formality. Each county stuck to its traditional methods as practised by the local builder. The axial stack was never popular in stone building areas; more often it was formed in the same gable-end as the front door. In the Devon mud or 'cob' cottage, the 'front chimney' was usual, and generally speaking it was West-country practice to build the main chimney stack on a side wall near the front door.

When London was rebuilt after the Great Fire in 1666 the number of chimneys increased enormously. Flues were made smaller and were usually built in the party walls with projecting chimney breasts, the roof-top chimney being in brick, finished with two or three projecting courses, or perhaps a course of tiles. By this time coal had become scarcer and dearer, chiefly because of the Dutch fleet's activities in the Thames which prevented colliers from Newcastle landing their cargoes. On top of that, in 1670 the Government decided to increase the coal tax to help pay for the rebuilding of fifty-two City churches destroyed in the fire. But the nuisance of coal smoke, fast becoming an urgent problem does not seem to have been diminished, however.

There was an attempt to produce smokeless fuel in 1656, in which John Evelyn took the closest interest. He saw John Winter's scheme of 'charring sea-cole, to burn without sulphur and render it sweete'. He also proposed that the trades which produced this 'fuliginous and filthy vapour' should be removed from the confines of the city, but nothing came of it. It is possible that much of the trouble was caused by the chimneys not being high enough to take the smoke away, a fact not fully appreciated at that time.

The design of chimneys changed little in the ensuing centuries, but the problem of smoking remained. There were many experiments with ventilating fireplaces which had a complicated system of pipes and flues, but the simple idea of opening a window to provide air was frowned upon. One nineteenth-century architect declared that such a step would be 'at the peril of the occupants of the room.' He further stated that a smoky chimney would be cured at once, and a complete ventilation of the room could be effected, by the use of a simple valve.

The truth is that a chimney will smoke under certain conditions: when the top is surrounded by air condensed by pressure, while the air below is in its normal state. This happens when a chimney stands near an object higher than itself. A strong gust of wind may strike the object without touching the chimney itself, and by its pressure condense the air below it and drive it down the mouth of the chimney and in any other direction where no resistance is offered. This is understood today, and the problem is usually dealt with by fitting a type of cowl on the chimney pot to meet the particular situation. The north of England cottager, clinging to his 'longhouse' with squat chimneys, had his own method of combating a down draught. He simply fixed two pieces of flat stone together to form a V-shape on top of the chimney.

The success of any open fire depends upon the construction of the flues, as well as the chimney. Modern science can answer many of those flue problems which Count Rumford and others found so baffling 150 years ago, and we know that for the efficient operation of the fire it is essential to have a smooth, funnel-shaped 'gather' that begins at the top of the opening and gradually tapers into the chimney proper.

Page 114 shows the accepted way of fixing a fireplace according to the British Standard Code of Practice C.P.131.101, formulated in 1951, and so far not bettered.

Chimneys built after 1965 were required by the new Building Regulations to be lined either with salt-glazed pipes or with some kind of pre-cast liner. A chimney built before that date can often be substantially improved by the use of a new lining system.

The development of a prefabricated chimney has brought great advances to flue efficiency and it has a life as long as the house itself. In addition to allowing the replacement of an existing chimney, it means that an open fire can be introduced into a room – or a house – where there is at present no chimney. These prefabricated chimneys are

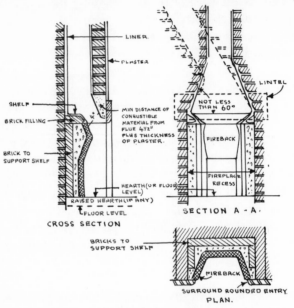

32 The accepted way of fixing a fireplace

insulated with metal or ceramic liners to ensure even temperatures through the whole length of the flue, and that means that the fires they serve will burn more brightly, and there will be no chimney maintenance needed, apart from the occasional sweep.

This is a far cry from the medieval smoke hole, but on the way down the centuries the chimney has lost its decorative appearance. From the beginning of the twentieth century onwards domestic chimneys have been made in plain rough-cast, with stone caps or earthenware chimney pots – no longer an important element of a design, but built with strict regard to economy.

10

Fireplace Furniture

When man learned to use fire in his domestic quarters he also devised the means of containing it within a safe, limited area and invented implements to aid combustion and to help with his cooking preparations.

Before the advent of the machine many of these implements were designed and embellished with a real sense of craftsmanship and a certain rugged kind of beauty.

Andirons

One of the earliest of these inventions is variously known as the andiron or endiron (the brand iron in Sussex), but perhaps its commonest name is simply the firedog, though the origin of that expressive word is obscure. It is one of a pair of iron supports for logs in an open fireplace, so that the ends of the brands can be raised to allow the passage of air between them. It also kept the burning logs from rolling out into the room.

The origin of these 'ancient twin servitors of the hearth' is lost in antiquity. We see them in early manuscripts as having straddle legs with hooks in front to rest the spit irons upon, the standards ending in a scroll something like a shepherd's crook. These were of wrought iron, showing a very high standard of craftsmanship at that time. In fact, these simple designs continued to be made by village smiths for as long as people burnt logs and that might well be up to the present day in some country districts. They were eminently satisfactory and full of a character that was expressive of the craftsman's own ideas rather than taken from a design put down on paper. The very few medieval firedogs that remain are of course of great antiquarian value.

Firedogs coupled in the manner of those in the fourteenth-century Great Hall at Penshurst Place are also rare (see page 12). Here the massive double trestle of cast iron was specially made to take huge burning logs, and each stanchion is embossed with the coat of arms of the Sidneys. They were probably made in the time of Edward VI and are immensely strong and durable as their present good condition shows.

Firedogs came into general use at the end of the fifteenth century, following the French fashion. In the kitchen they were strong and massive but usually quite plain. They were equally massive in the hall, to support the enormous fires, but much more ornamental. Some had brass rings, knobs, rosettes and various grotesque forms to decorate them, and the crook head was superseded by a cup-shaped top (page 117), which was a cresset for holding a light; spit hooks were still in evidence.

As a rule, English firedogs were tall, elaborate and lavishly ornamented, especially during the reign of Henry VIII, but they became smaller and simpler in design in Elizabethan and Jacobean times until they eventually became unnecessary and obsolete by the end of the seventeenth century.

When ironfounding was developed in the Weald of Sussex at the beginning of the sixteenth century, cast-iron firedogs became one of the most important manufactures, and because of the variety of design they made a welcome, artistic addition to the open hearth. Models had to be made in sand, so designs were often repeated. The most characteristic form had an arched base supporting a column, caryatid or figure, or (page 117) the English lion and the Tudor rose, with the rose repeated on the feet. A shield covered the intersection of the standard with the billet bar and this very often bore the sacred monogram.

In the drawing-room at Loseley we see the tall downward-tapering pillar with voluted head, after the style that was commonly used in wood; but by contrast, those in the dining-room have upward-tapering pillars with ball finials.

Firedogs were a favourite place to display a family symbol. The bittern from the Lytton family crest is seen at Knebworth proudly perched on more than one pair of firedogs, as a striking finial. It is said that Cardinal Wolsey had cardinals' hats on some of his firedogs at Hampton Court Palace. In an inventory of his furniture there are no fewer than forty-seven pairs of andirons mentioned, all of them lavishly ornamented.

a   b   c

33 (a) wrought-iron firedog, with spit hooks and cresset bowl top; (b) cast-iron firedog, featuring the English lion and the Tudor rose, common in the sixteenth century; (c) cherub on firedog, often encased in silver on an iron base – seventeenth century

Many designs fuse Gothic and Renaissance styles, which the iron-founder used to good effect; nevertheless, cast iron was not thought to be good enough for the owners of the great houses of the sixteenth and seventeenth centuries, and we find a considerable variety made in more costly metals. The bases and working parts continued to be iron, with brass, silver and silver-gilt used for decoration in the standards and finial and the spit hooks disappeared. The cherub (as in drawing C above) was often made in silver on an iron base encased in silver, and some were richly embossed.

The standards gave the Renaissance sculptor the opportunity for great play in imagination and line and he indulged it to the full. The Stuart period, in particular, gave us some very beautiful examples. In King William's room at Hampton Court Palace are a pair of silver gilt andirons, 16½in high, which are attributed to Andrew Moore, 1696–7. They are truly splendid pieces.

Elaborate French and Italian andirons were imported into England at this time, some examples of which are seen at Wilton House, Salisbury, and the tapestry room at Ham House, Surrey.

The general luxury of the Restoration period was reflected, very typically, in the design and accoutrements of the fireplace, which began to be ornamented in embossed silver, but on the whole it was so well done that it never looked ostentatious or out of place. At Ham House some unusual fire pans for burning charcoal are encased in embossed silver. In the pan stand firedogs with small figure finials, also of silver. The addition of these dogs meant that logs could be used if desired. A type of enamelled firedog from that time was made basically of cast brass with the depressions in the ornamentation encrusted in enamel, mainly in green, blue, red and white. The Victoria & Albert Museum display some perfect examples of this kind of art.

When coal came into general use firedogs were no longer necessary. With them went a great deal of the character and the charm of the open fireplace.

Firebacks

Many of the accoutrements of the fireplace and the grate were works of art in their own right, and this is particularly true of the fireback which quite literally gave our ancestors 'pictures in the fire'.

Metal firebacks first came into use about the end of the fifteenth century. Their purpose was to protect the brickwork at the back of the open fireplace from the fierce heat of the flames. They also helped to throw the heat into the room. As coal began to replace wood, especially in towns, they became even more necessary and by the middle of the seventeenth century were in general use, making a very picturesque addition to the hearth.

34 Seventeenth-century fireback in cast-iron, showing a crowned lion with thistle, fleur-de-lys and Tudor rose – always a popular motif
35 Eighteenth-century stoveback of classical design

At first they were cast by pressing a wooden board, the size of the back required, into a bed of loam or sand. Various decorative objects were pressed into the mould, then molten iron was poured in and allowed to cool, when the decoration appeared in low relief in the casting.

Some of the earliest firebacks were simply rectangular slabs of cast iron and the first attempts at decoration were crude but nonetheless effective. A sword, a pair of compasses, a rose, some scissors and a knife, or even the impress of a workman's hand might be used – it seems as if the first thing to hand was picked up and pressed into the sand.

The use of rope, hardened with glue and pressed down into the mould, was a favourite method of producing a pattern of sorts, with a rope edging. Short lengths were also used to make the sign of the cross, partly for decoration but more often as a device to keep evil spirits

away. Grave slabs were frequently used as a mould to commemorate a
death in the family. In many respects the fireplace seems to have been a
favourite site for a memorial of any kind, possibly because it was the
central point in a room.

Early firebacks were made with movable stamps, forming small
separate decorative motifs. As a rule, those impressed with a single
wooden panel denote a fireback of later date.

36 A fireback of Dutch origin, with the typical arched top and dolphins
reclining on either side

There were three distinct types, the earliest (fifteenth and early
sixteenth century) having the width greater than the height; the middle
type (seventeenth century, overlapping to sixteenth and eighteenth)
with width and height about equal; and the later type (mostly eighteenth
century), the stove back, being higher than it was wide. The elaborate
decoration of these later ones was due to Flemish and Dutch influence
which tended to be much more ornate than English. Firebacks imported
from Holland were copied in England, and some very beautiful designs
were seen at this time, with the typical arched top and dolphins reclining
on either side.

Of the English ones, a great number were produced at ironworks in
Sussex, which was at one time the centre of the charcoal-burning

industry supplying essential fuel to the neighbouring ironfounding counties. Today, the finest collection of domestic ironwork is housed at Lewes, at Anne of Cleves House, Southover, now a museum run by the Sussex Archaeological Society. Among their rarities are two early fireback moulds of wood, probably the only ones left in the country

37 Sixteenth-century fireback displaying a family crest and motto

There is also an interesting panel scene showing an ironworks and tools of the trade, belonging to the Carron Company, and a runner and duct which was used to convey liquid metal into the mould.

A browse round this museum shows that some of the most popular decorative designs at any time represented the arms of the reigning sovereigns, from Henry VII to James II. Some of these may also be seen in Hampton Court Palace, and more occasionally one comes across one in an old country house.

Wealthy people entitled to their own coat of arms would have them specially cast, those of humbler birth would add their own initials to a standard design, to give a personal touch. A coat of arms on a plain back, or just initials, were peculiarly English. The more flamboyant designs usually originated elsewhere.

Biblical themes were popular in any country. A German fireback of the seventeenth century uses Moses and the serpent in the wilderness. Sometimes the characters were shown wearing contemporary dress, and it was not unusual to see Old Testament figures in Tudor armour and the Virgin in a ruff. The Lewes museum has a fireback with scenes from the Book of Esther impressed with a single wooden panel. The work and craftsmanship involved was considerable to produce such detail.

Current events were also commemorated by a suitable fireback design. Some of the best known of these were made after the defeat of the Armada, having an anchor, fleur-de-lys and roses in the centre panel and the date 1588 in a prominent position. The Boscobel Oak is another very well-known design, showing the tree in which King Charles II is said to have taken refuge after the Battle of Worcester. A further design symbolised his Restoration in 1661, with the legendary phoenix proclaiming the rebirth of the monarchy.

There was a seemingly endless variation of themes both quaint and beautiful and when the fireplace became smaller and the size of the grate diminished, their passing, like that of the old firedogs, took with them some of the individuality and picturesqueness of the open fireplace.

Cast-iron firebacks are too heavy and cumbersome to become popular as collectors' pieces, and for this reason a good many of them must have been destroyed or lost, though obviously some have been rescued by museums. Fortunately there has been a revival of interest of late by antiquarians who realise their historic value. Some architectural ironmongers are also reproducing designs in firebacks to complement the period fireplaces that are coming back into fashion.

A wooden pattern after the style of that used by the moulder for the fireback was also used for casting a 'turf plate', a large flat cast-iron platform used to raise the fire a few inches above floor level. It took its name from the fuel that was most used, and was seen in North Yorkshire more than anywhere else.

Firebaskets and Grates

The firebasket was introduced during the seventeenth century for the purpose of burning sea coal. It was an openwork container, cauldron shape, usually constructed of iron bars and made to stand on a hearth. Some of the early ones were made large enough to take logs as an alternative to coal and these generally had spikes along the top to keep the logs from falling out. There is a particularly fine firebasket in the double-cube room at Wilton House, standing high up on scrolled feet. Sometimes grates of this kind were intended to be portable, but they must have been cumbersome to move around.

Designers concentrated mainly upon improvement of shape and style for sitting-rooms, and many attractive models were produced during the latter part of the seventeenth century. By about the middle of the eighteenth century the cast-iron grate was built into the fireplace and raised above the hearth, leaving a space into which the ashes dropped. At first it was set between two brick hobs which later became two cast-iron panels, suitably ornamented, the forerunner of the cooking grate.

Some of the early types showed marked French influence in their decoration before the more formal style of the Adam brothers was adopted. Typical of the latter part of the eighteenth century was a firebasket with rounded or bowed bars, side panels and a pierced apron, the opening enclosed by a frame. These were ornamented in great detail and were given fenders to match, making a very pleasing set.

The most beautiful basket or detached grates were designed by the Adams, made to complement their chimneypieces, with fronts superbly modelled and chased. Some designs for these grates may be seen in the Adams' collection in the Soane Museum.

A sarcophagus-type grate was also introduced about this time, much heavier to look at, though the design suited some of the massive chimneypieces with which it was used. Its chief feature was its substantial side supports of cast-iron, sometimes enriched with honeysuckle ornament and brass claw feet.

Grates of each period are also discussed in detail in their relevant chapters, since in most cases they merge in with the general design of a fireplace.

Early in the nineteenth century fireplace openings were completely filled with iron plate and an arched opening displayed the grate. This was the first 'interior', which afterwards became the standard way of furnishing the fireplace.

Fire Irons

By this term we usually mean shovel, tongs, poker, log fork, etc, implements which came into more general use in the eighteenth century as coal supplanted all other types of fuel. They were long-handled, for protection from the flames, and usually rested against standards in the hearth. They were practical tools but, being made by craftsmen, were usually decorative. In the average home they were made of steel or, more frequently, brass, and all needed hand cleaning. In the homes of the wealthy they were given greater importance by silver mountings incorporating the family crest and insignia, as were those at Burghley House (Chapter 6).

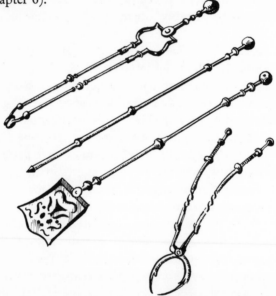

38 Seventeenth-century fire irons and early tongs for logs

That fire irons of this kind were in use before the eighteenth century is borne out by items in an inventory of the contents of the green drawing-room at Ham House in 1679: 'One Iron Back, one fire pan with two dogs and fire shovell and tongues garnisht with silver. One broome and one bellowes garnisht with silver. Two silver hooks. One silver hearth rodd.'

This drawing-room was originally known as the Queen's bedchamber. It was prepared for a visit by Charles II's Queen, Catherine of Braganza, some time during the late seventeenth century, which accounts for the lavish display of silver ornamentation. The embossed silver firepan incorporates the Duchess of Lauderdale's cypher in its scrolling foliage. It was used for the burning of charcoal, but dogs were also provided for use if a log fire was preferred. It may also have been used as a perfuming pan, for burning charcoal with a piece of rosin or fircone on the embers to sweeten the air. A 'perfuming panne' is an item found in many old inventories.

The bellows hanging by the side of the fireplace are particularly beautiful, overlaid with embossed and chased silver on one side and decorated with marquetry on the other. It was this lovely silver 'chimney furniture' that caught the eye of Horace Walpole when he visited Ham House in 1770 after his niece married the fifth Earl of Dysart. Though the rooms are relatively small, this scrupulous attention to detail and refinement makes them appear luxurious.

With the coming of the twentieth century, tall fire irons began to go out of favour, and as labour-saving fireplaces replaced the high Victorian grates, so the fire irons were reduced in size until they became what we now call a 'companion set', consisting of a small hearth-brush, shovel, tongs and poker hung around a central stand. Variations of this set are used where the open fire is favoured, but they are made from metals that are either oxidised or lacquered, needing no more than the rub of a duster to keep them bright, and exhibit not a touch of originality.

Fenders

With the establishment of coal-burning grates, fenders became a part of fireplace tradition, necessary to confine the ashes within safe limits. Far from being purely utilitarian and featureless, they were made as ornamental as possible, often matching the apron of the grate or, especially where Adam was concerned, all of a piece with the general décor of a room. Like the fire irons they were made basically of steel or brass, often with bands of stamped, pierced ornament around them, kept highly polished. At Burghley House the silver mountings on the fireplaces are repeated on the fenders which are imposing enough to warrant this unusual treatment.

For large marble hearths, low, pierced fenders without return were usual. For smaller hearths the fenders were taller, with bottom plates and feet. It was not until after World War I that tiled kerbs were introduced and eventually took the place of the decorative metal fender.

Coal Scuttles

The first receptacles for coal were quite attractive to look at, and were usually made of gleaming copper or brass. The old helmet-shape scuttle was about the most popular in the average home. It was superseded by a simple container with a lid, made of oxidised silver or copper, to save cleaning.

11

A Variety of Materials

A very wide range of materials is used in the construction and decoration of fireplaces today. In fact, given the proviso that the parts nearest the fire must be incombustible, almost anything goes; but before the days of easy transport for craftsmen and materials it was not always so. Our ancestors took great pains to exploit to the full the materials found in their immediate neighbourhood, with the result that regional characteristics became very marked and a highly individual style of building was developed in each area.

Stone

This applies particularly to stone, the oldest and most enduring building material of all, with a natural beauty that is characteristic of the county in which it is found. One has only to think of York stone and Scottish granite to appreciate the analogy.

The fourteenth-century stone mason was, in effect, an architect as well as a sculptor, and we can trace this combination of skills in some of the old stone fireplaces still surviving. He knew his stone intimately and how to 'work' it to the best advantage. The modern mason must combine a practical knowledge of geology with the science of building in order to understand the different methods involved in shaping and dressing the various kinds of stone, each in the past confined to its own region. There are the flints and chalks of East Anglia, the sandstones of parts of the Midlands and Yorkshire, the granites of the north and west, with a great belt of limestone in between, running through Dorset, east Somerset, Gloucestershire, north Wiltshire, Oxfordshire, North-ampton, Leicestershire and Nottinghamshire to east Yorkshire; it is this limestone which produces some of the finest building material in the world – Kentish rag, Portland stone, Caen stone, Bath stone and so on.

Stone of course offers a great variation in colour and texture. It may be almost white, creamy, yellow, grey, brown, red or nearly black, according to the mineral content, and the mason knows how to 'work' each one to emphasise its individual characteristics and to bring out its colour and markings. Some markings, as in muresque stone, are made by fossilised organic matter, others, as in Northamptonshire stone, are coloured by ironstone or a variety of quartz. Riven stone, 'hammer dressed' or with 'chopped face', made as accurate as the tool permits, has a rough natural beauty which adapts to any setting. Fine rubbed and sawn stone are alternative choices, and certain kinds of very hard stone, like Purbeck, lend themselves to polishing, like marble. There is also a 'reconstructed' stone, which is much used for modern fireplaces and is sometimes preferred for its unbroken smoothness.

We usually associate granite with the monumental mason, but it is used to a certain extent for fireplaces. In the less sophisticated parts of the West-country small cottages would often have a fireplace consisting of two large stone slabs with another slab for a lintel, standing on a raised hearth. The extreme hardness of local granite made it suitable for this purpose. It can also be decorative, being composed of a jumbled mass of tiny mineral crystals, some of which are distinguishable as felspar, mica and quartz – white or grey or pink – giving a speckled effect. When smoothed and polished it has a very attractive appearance, and looks good as an inlay. Adam used Scottish granite inlays on a white marble chimneypiece in the great drawing-room at Burghley House, Stamford.

The granites of different regions vary so much in colour, composition and texture, 'shading off' into other rocks almost imperceptibly, that other names are appropriate for them. Where a number of large mineral crystals predominate, it is called porphyry, from the Greek word for 'purple'. The name was originally given to a reddish ornamental Egyptian stone, much used for decoration in times past. It forms part of the ornamentation of the white marble chimneypiece in the state bedroom at Burghley House – possibly the royal purple was used as a compliment to the royal guests who were entertained there.

There are many stones that can be used for decoration in this fashion, but they are rarely used imaginatively these days. Though stone used to be regarded as the rich man's material, that is no longer true, for its cost compares favourably with other materials. A natural stone fireplace fits as easily into the modern room as did the great carved stone chimney-pieces in the Norman castle or medieval manor.

Bricks

Bricks were not used in any quantity until the time of the Tudors, when the less well-to-do people began to build fireplaces in brick to imitate those of stone in the lord's great house. Elaborate brick chimney stacks also made their appearance. Those early bricks varied a great deal in size, from 8 to 11in long, $3\frac{3}{4}$ to 6in wide and $1\frac{1}{4}$ to 2in thick. At first they were like Roman bricks, laid irregularly, until regular bonding was introduced early in the fifteenth century and brick sizes began to follow Flemish dimensions. The bricks themselves were of rough texture, rather uneven in shape and size, a beautiful warm rosy colour. They were laid with thick mortar joints. Some parts of a fireplace were made of moulded bricks – fired in a mould to a special shape to form a mould or ornament. They were sometimes plastered over to imitate stonework.

Sizes of bricks began to increase towards the end of the seventeenth century, when moulded brickwork was replaced by specially made soft bricks carved and cut to contemporary Renaissance designs. It re-appeared later in the nineteenth century in a variety of designs, and there was another brief revival in the early twentieth century, when narrow bricks moulded after the Tudor style were sometimes used. This tradition lingers in the special briquettes made for modern fireplaces, which are roughly $6 \times 3 \times 1\frac{1}{2}$ or 2in, sandfaced and dirt-resistant. Bricks fired at a high temperature are practically imperishable and because they also retain the heat they are the ideal material for fireplaces. Many fine old Tudor brick hole-in-the-wall fireplaces are still in existence, proof enough of the lasting quality of the materials.

Stucco

Stucco is a fine plaster used for architectural decoration, made to look like stone. It was known to the ancients and freely used in Italy in the sixteenth century. The Italians employed by Henry VIII at his palace of Nonsuch, Surrey, introduced this form of plasterwork into England and it developed during the reign of Elizabeth and the Stuarts. From simple incised pargeting came the ornamentation in relief that seems to bear some relationship to sculpture and wood carving.

39 An early example of a stucco chimneypiece, in the Wynne Room at Plas Mawr, Conway

The fine plaster used for moulded and decorated overmantels was often floated in a thick coating on to a 'keyed' base over laths on battens. The work was done very quickly while the plaster was wet, to avoid cracking, and the most intricate of patterns were achieved with simple, homely tools such as the country plasterer still uses to-day. For repeating ornaments, casts were made and set up, but in the main the stuccoist worked to his own designs, using his own methods, so there are probably no two plaster chimneypieces that look alike. Understandably, the wall over the fireplace presented an inviting background for the art of the sixteenth-century stuccoist and many important homes were decorated in this fashion. The photograph (shown opposite) shows an interesting early example at Plas Mawr, Conway, the date 1577 inscribed on it being the year the place was built by Robert Wynne.

In other houses splendid heraldic devices were emblazoned on the chimneypieces, some brightly coloured to make a magnificent focal point. Designs of classical or scriptural significance were also fairly common in Elizabethan times. Shakespeare mentions a fireplace with a painted chimneypiece in *Cymbeline,* in a description of Imogen's chamber: 'The chimney is south the chamber; and the chimneypiece chaste Dian, bathing. . . .' In those colourful days many chimneypieces were painted and gilded and it was difficult to tell whether they were plaster or stone.

Though the art has generally died out, there are still craftsmen who are skilled in ornamental plasterwork, able to carry out faithful restorations to old stucco chimneypieces.

Marble

The early Renaissance saw the beginning of the fashion for marble chimneypieces, inspired, no doubt, by the craze for all things Italian. By the time of the reign of Queen Anne, French marble chimneypieces were imported into England and marble became a trade article in the eighteenth-century.

'Marble' is, in fact, a loose term embracing any limestone in its hardest and most crystalline form which is capable of being polished. For this reason master masons and sculptors found in it the ideal material from which to produce their masterpieces, and many splendid carvings were executed by well-known artists for chimneypieces during the long period of the Renaissance. Many of these have been described elsewhere in the text and it is true to say that there are few great houses of this time without some notable examples of carved marble chimneypieces.

Of the many varieties of marble obtainable, white is the purest and rarest. It was used by Grecian sculptors in their statues from about 568 BC and has been coveted ever since. The finest varieties of white marble come from the Italian quarries at Carrara, and this was the kind used by Inigo Jones for some of his famous chimneypieces at Wilton House, Salisbury. They were carved in Italy before being brought to Wilton to complement the classical Palladian style of the rooms for which they were designed.

Clouded white marbles are much more abundant than the pure white, and the best varieties are even more durable than granite. Mantels of this kind of marble graced many prosperous middle-class homes especially in Victorian times.

Some of the black marbles have a dramatic effect – the 'paragone' of Bergamo is a fine black, the 'portor' from Genoa is beautifully veined with yellow, and in between the blacks and the whites are the coloured and variegated marbles which have a rare beauty when polished. Today the marbles ranging from beige and shades of grey to deep olive green, each with its distinctive markings are in favour, and most of them can be used together quite naturally. A rich effect is obtained by inlaying the ground of the ornament with marble of a different colour – at which the craftsmen of the early Renaissance were highly skilled. There is a fine specimen of Italian craftsmanship of this kind in the Victoria & Albert Museum, a large imposing chimneypiece in green and white marble, inlaid with coloured marble, made in the early sixteenth-century workshop of Riccio, Padua. It is not known in which house it originally stood.

Adam often used coloured marble inlays on white statuary marble (see Chapter 6), with a liking for yellow sienna (yellow with large purplish spots or veins) and verde-antique (a clouded green).

Highly polished alabaster was also used as a form of decoration, as at Bolsover Castle. It is a soft crystalline form of sulphate of lime, or granulated gypsum, white and translucent. That in greatest repute among the ancients came from Alabastron in Egypt. Nowadays we are more likely to get it from places on the Kent coast or the Midlands, where gypsum forms beds several feet thick.

Onyx is usually thought of as an ornamental semi-pellucid stone of the quartz family, but there is in fact an onyx marble which is much used for fireplaces – more often in the form of inset panels to contrast with something like Portuguese beige polished marble, or similar. Or it is sometimes seen as an interior with a wood mantel. Its variously coloured veins – caused by layers of chalcedony – and the play of colours are singularly beautiful. The kind of onyx used for modern fireplaces mostly comes from Turkey and Pakistan.

Marbles are also imported from Italy, France, Greece and Portugal in tremendous variety. Rustic marble, in rough-faced strips, is a pleasing alternative to the polished kind; its subtle shades are, if anything, more pronounced. Riven marble can also be polished to bring out its natural beauty. The modern equivalent of hand-carved decorations on marble chimneypieces is a simple hand-etched frieze, which is equally attractive in its own idiom.

Scagliola

Imitation marble, known as scagliola, was introduced by Italian artificers during the Adam period. It was made by mixing a specially prepared hard plaster with pieces of marble, the whole being rubbed down and polished to produce the effect of real marble. It was used a great deal for columns and pilasters in important eighteenth-century houses, and in the ornamentation of fireplaces. In this context its use became an art in its own right. There is an excellent example in the Victoria & Albert Museum, where a white marble chimneypiece is shown inlaid with this coloured composition in a design of trailing leaves. The effect is beautiful and naturalistic. .

The earliest examples of the use of scagliola on chimneypieces in England may be seen at Ham House, Surrey, and Castle Howard, Yorkshire, both of which are described in detail in Chapter 6. Scagliola is still used to-day and is in demand for restoration work. To the untutored eye, it is difficult to tell from real marble.

Wood

Wood has been a popular material for chimneypieces from the earliest times. There was a great development in joiners' crafts during the early Renaissance period, and from being comparatively rare, oak chimneypieces became commonplace in Jacobean times, elaborately carved after the Italian style rather than the Flemish.

Many Italians came to England at this time and they must often have worked side by side with English wood carvers, learning from each other. The Italians brought their tools with them and to this day the wood-carver's tools bear a quaint mixture of English and Italian names. The Italians' work was light in touch and often extravagantly embellished, with Renaissance influence obvious in much of the details and mouldings of the chimneypieces, but it was not long before an English style began to prevail, showing a suitable treatment of the fine old oak of which they were made. Some Jacobean chimneypieces show a form of marquetry, in which thin layers of coloured woods were wrought into a design.

Because of the profligate use of English oak for everything from fuel to building, there was as we have seen a great shortage by the time of the seventeenth-century, and imported softwoods began to be used. Pine became a favourite with the wood carvers who found it softer to work than oak. Some fine pinewood chimneypieces were carved at this time, showing a wealth of detailed ornamentation.

A great many reproduction chimneypieces in pine are produced to-day, and for this the wood is treated by a process of dipping, staining and bleaching to take the newness out of it. Then it is waxed and burnished to give it a satin lustre and to bring out the colour of the wood. This helps to give a wholly authentic appearance to a reproduction piece.

For very detailed enrichments lime is preferred for its finer grain. Grinling Gibbons' carvings were in lime – he rarely used anything else. For chimneypieces the completed carvings were glued and pinned on, with the pins hammered home in a part of the design where they are unseen. Reproduction wood carvers use exactly the same techniques now, Grinling Gibbons' methods never having been bettered.

The brothers Adam often used wood for their less important chimneypieces, probably pine, then coming into use fairly generally. The Adams had many followers and there were many wood carvers who were well able to follow their style – a charming, graceful style that linked the fireplace with the interior decoration as a whole.

Some of Robert Adam's applied ornamentation is not carved wood, though it looks like it. It is in fact a composition pressed into moulds. When he was seeking a quicker and cheaper means of producing applied ornamentation for his designs for interiors he bought this famous recipe for composition from Liardet, the Swiss pastor, and entrusted it to George Jackson, of Rathbone Place, London, who carved reverse moulds in boxwood and pressed out the ornament in this material. It was much less expensive than carved wood, but it had the disadvantage of being difficult to strip down when painted and inevitably some of the fine detail was lost. These moulds and the composition are still used by Jackson's to-day, their collection running into many thousands. Now a flourishing firm in Hammersmith, London, it owes its foundation to Robert Adam's initiative almost two hundred years ago.

The fashion set by Adam has never really died out. Carved pine mantels are in fashion at present, either with composition ornament for painting, or in hand-carved waxed pine. Whitewood mantels primed for painting are also a popular trade article. Mahogany, oak, African teak and other suitable woods have their place among modern materials; a sleek, streamlined effect is sometimes obtained by using blockboard with a teak or mahogany finish achieved by a veneer simulation process.

Ceramic Tiles

Ceramic tiles appeal to many people for their ease of cleaning and maintenance, as well as their traditional beauty. Back in the eighteenth century, tiles were a status symbol. Dutch tiles, with their traditional blue and white colouring, were much sought after and are indeed very rare now. The Ancient House, Ipswich, has some representing Palleas and Mars, in the original lining to one of their fireplaces.

Some very beautiful ceramic tiles were designed during the Victorian period, either for the whole fireplace or for the reveals, as at Knebworth House, Herts. The last part of the nineteenth century saw the beginnings of what was called 'art pottery', and offshoot of the Arts and Crafts Movement inspired by William Morris. The most influential art potter at this time was William de Morgan, who revived the use of lustre colours and 'Persian' colours. He made decorative tiles from his own designs at his Fulham Sands End Pottery between 1888 and 1898 which were the delight of the aesthetes and greatly admired in artistic circles. Some of his blue and white tiles bearing a simple floral design are seen in the Hunting Room at Clandon Park, Surrey, where they form the sides of the fireplace. They were probably put there when the fireplace was projected forwards into the room to make it more efficient.

Some other art potters at that time reflected the Japanese influences of the 1870s and 1880s and there was already a suggestion of what was to be called Art Nouveau. Picture tiles of this period are now collectors' pieces.

Victorian ceramic art is seen at its most beautiful in the fireplace shown on page 91. It is in Turiness embossed ceramic tiles with a polished wood mantelshelf. As a direct contrast there is a comparatively simple fireplace with enamelled copper tiled surround set up in the Victoria & Albert Museum. It was designed by C. R. Ashbee (1863–1942) and executed by Arthur Cameron, 1893. This fireplace was taken from the entrance hall of the Magpie and Stump, Chelsea, and makes an interesting comparison with some of the more lavishly decorated ones of that period.

It was wholly regrettable when the ugly fashions of the early part of this century swept away the attractive Victorian tiles and substituted plain slab ones. Fortunately, there is now a renewal of appreciation of the traditional beauty of ceramics, and the dull, porridge-coloured slab has been replaced by its silk-screen printed and textured modern counterpart, made from clays which give it special strength. Plain, embossed or incised, these ceramics are a feature in their own right and give tremendous scope to the fireplace designer. Time will not fade the colours and since they are both fireproof and stainproof there can hardly be a more suitable material for a fireplace surround. Hand-carved or hand-painted tiles add a touch of distinction to an individual design and may well prove to be a profitable investment for the future.

Ceramics or marble in the form of mosaics have a wide appeal and blend well with modern designs.

Red quarry tiles have always been with us, appreciated for their homeliness and hard-wearing qualities. They are still a favourite material for hearths, and when well polished give a warm glow to the family fireplace.

Slate

Slate has come into its own as a decorative material. There are now many colourful varieties available – natural, restful shades of silver grey, seal grey, gunmetal, Westmorland green, or multi-colour. There are also some beautiful colours among the South African slates. All can be highly polished or left in the riven state; either way slate is excellent material for fireplace surrounds or hearths.

Metal

Metals of various kinds are used very skilfully by modern designers to bring the fireplace's image into the space age. Vitreous enamel on cast iron has long been used to produce a lustre finish in bronze, copper and other suitable colours. Now, some of the latest designs use strong, bright colours for stove enamelling on iron, to make a vivid focal point of an unusual fireplace. Decorative features are made from cast bronze and alloys and these look well in a ceramic tile surround, but there are, of course, many variations on this theme. Cast-brass enrichments, canopies, frames and panels in stainless steel, satin chrome, armour bright or copper often give a new look to a traditional design, and wrought-iron gates and frame in black enamel may enclose a fire opening or a recess for logs, etc.

Perhaps the most dramatic break-through in the exploitation of metals here is with stainless steel. A colouring process has recently been developed which has greatly augmented its natural good qualities of long life, resistance to corrosion and ease of maintenance. After extensive research at the European Research and Development Laboratories of International Nickel Ltd, in Birmingham, a simple operational process was developed whereby the metal can assume the basic colours of blue, gold, red and green, with subtle variations of each shade. These colours add to the appeal of stainless steel whilst still preserving its characteristic metallic lustre.

With such a wide choice of materials available and the almost unlimited combinations possible with them, it is a wonder that so many people are satisfied with some of the dull, uninspiring fireplaces that are still seen around to-day. Given a touch of originality and a sense of artistry the fireplace could be transformed into the beautiful, eye-catching central feature that it was in past ages.

12

The Fireplace Today

We have now passed through the phase of rejecting open fires completely, and a majority of homes at least have an open fire in the living room, even if the rest of the house relies on central heating or portable electric fires.

We have also rejected those designers who decided that beauty must go unless it was labour-saving. Others have taken their place who see the fireplace in terms of an artistic creation – dignified, striking or even bizarre if the room demands it. The end result is the same – to create a focal point, to bring a room to life, to reject a clinical sterility that does nothing for anyone. The aesthetic pleasure of a leaping, living fire is intensified by a feeling of security when other means of power are threatened – a hazard which seems to have become a regular feature of modern life.

So history has come full circle. We have seen the early central hearth, the medieval chimneypiece 'set in a frayme of wood', followed by the heraldic panel, the sculptured bas-relief, the moral maxim, the scriptural and classical subjects, the towering overmantel and mirror and the nondescript all-tile fireplace. Now we are back to the central fire, the hole-in-the-wall and the overpiece in modern guise. We are experiencing a renaissance of the open fire and a great upsurge of interest in its design.

The fireplace received a fillip at the time of the Festival of Britain in 1951, when manufacturers succeeded in getting some interesting designs

40 Modern 'hole in the wall', made by Bell. Framed in stainless steel, copper or bronze, with decorative canopy. The log-box hearth has a marble or slate sectional top

accepted. The Council of Industrial Design also approved several new designs for fireplace tiles, bringing this somewhat neglected field of ceramic art into the public eye once more. By and large, it is a successful choice from the varied materials available today that makes an interesting and attractive fireplace.

The trend towards the use of natural materials drifted over to Britain from the Continent about ten or fifteen years ago, and it brought with it a wonderful range of marble, both riven and polished, slate in its varying colours, stone, quartzite and onyx, stimulating designers to fresh ideas. Interior decorators saw the different colour effects as the perfect foil to drapes, carpets and furniture generally.

Local materials, such as slate or stone, always look right in their regional settings. A builder in York made a special feature of individual fireplaces faced in York stone, and they were the prime attraction that sold the houses. In addition ceramic tiles, ceramic slate and ceramic marble were used to great effect to highlight the fireplace in schemes of interior decoration.

The recent trend towards the Georgian style of architecture calls for the classic beauty of the Adam fireplace. Consequently there is a great deal of reproduction work to be seen, with the traditional carved pine mantelpieces, dog grates, and firedogs. In the appropriate setting the style looks dignified and gives an air of distinction to a room of any size.

A great number of open-plan houses were built during the 1960s and many of the architects who recognised solid fuel as the most economical form of heating built fireplaces as an integral part of the structure. They were often made to furnish one end of a room, including recesses for logs, books, television set and even a deep window embrasure to take flower arrangements. Well-proportioned central chimney stacks were sometimes incorporated into their designs, with a fireplace set in the spine wall of the main living-room. This swing back to the old idea of a central chimney stack conserves heat lost through a conventionally sited stack.

One such house in the suburbs of London was ingeniously planned with a fireplace set in a brick spine wall which acted as a room divider. The fireplace was of polished stone with a single marble strip in the hearth to give it distinction. The grate had an air inlet and brick chamber under the floor. From this a hot-air vent ran to the dining area behind it and an outlet, through a pipe under a cupboard, went to the main bedroom above. Thus no heat was wasted, the house was warm and fuel consumption was cut to a minimum.

This kind of central fireplace was seen in many materials in the open-plan house. It was an important part of an architect's design, tailor-made to fit its surroundings. It accentuated the creation of two living spaces and acted as a focal point for two areas. It was also a display centre.

In one case, a living-room was planned around a simple open hearth and brick chimney. In another, the open hearth, occupying one entire wall, was faced in dull black slate, making a perfect foil for white curtains with a bold design of purple and black. People enjoyed interpreting their own ideas around a suitably dramatic focal point.

So the manufacturers began to cater for individual tastes, and in more traditional-style houses too the fireplace became once more the dominant feature of the living-room. There were designs to complement the long low look in interior design and others that soared to the ceiling in a modern version of a medieval chimneypiece, some using ceramic tiles with polished wood dividers in a new variation on a classic theme.

In between came the occasional design that stood on its own, belonging to no period, yet able to be slotted into any period without dis-

41 Fireplace in rustic marble, with hand-painted ceramic panels, a slate-top hearth and timber shelving. By Bell

harmony. One such fireplace was created specially for a small room, and made good use of glass: cloudy silvered mosaic glass made up the surround, while panels of glass above and around the chimneypiece added to the sparkling effect and gave the illusion of space that was so much needed.

Architects also made good use of split-level sites in the 1960s to produce houses that were distinctive in style with features that were a natural corollary of the ground available. In a house of this kind, built in 1961, a focal point was made of a free-standing fireplace which had a dramatic hexagonal cone of copper with a black wrought-iron brazier below and supporting piers of York stone. It was used to subdivide a large room; when the fire was not lit, the chimney could be sealed off to prevent the cold air streaming in. Broadly speaking, to-day's fireplace is an often delightful mixture of periods in modern dress.

The old idea of the central fire (never abandoned on the Continent) is fast gaining favour, and is ideal for a house with large rooms. The fire is brought out into the body of the room and usually built up off the ground, with a splendidly decorative hood and flue that descends from the ceiling. There is one of these circular fires in an apartment in

42 The modern version of the central fire, made basically in rustic marble and copper. By Bell

Paris where Sir Winston Churchill was once a frequent visitor. It has been much admired and copied many times. The fireplace illustrated (above) is basically in rustic marble, incorporating a 'Supaheat' fire base; the canopy is in copper and the chain-mail curtains in pewter finish. This kind of fireplace is suitable for party-givers, enabling the guests to circulate freely around it. It radiates the heat to every corner of the room and provides an interesting focal point. It is usually individually made.

There are many variations of this idea and most of them make use of canopies, or hoods – the early English answer to a smoking fire which is both practical and decorative – in copper, stainless steel, slate or ceramic tiles. One design uses Oriental lustre fine ceramic pieces in exclusive colours, complemented by white wall facings. Another has a canopy made in scored, textured and studded ceramic pieces in Roman bronze colour, foil for a moonstone-colour hearth with stone-effect edging. As a fourth wall feature ceramics have no rival and their colours are beautiful, giving full scope to originality.

43 One of the range of Claygate-Galleon fireplaces, the surround in multi-coloured briquettes with shelf and hearth in quarry tiles

It is precisely this wide choice of materials and design that gives the modern fireplace character and a certain panache. There is no longer any need for the householder to accept what the builder sends – as in the 1940s and early 1950s, when builders'-merchants' showrooms were full of dreary fireplaces in beige or brown tiles, sometimes hideously studded with coloured glass! The leading manufacturers now have their own designers and studio staff, who measure up and, if required, design a complete room-setting to include the fireplace, taking into account the proportions of a room and other essential details.

Conversions and Restoration
Many an old barn or coach house has been given a new lease of life

by an enthusiast who could visualise its potential worth. The installation of a new fireplace where none previously existed is a comparatively simple matter, though the work may need approval under the Building Regulations, and in this context a central fireplace with a cylindrical flue rising to the roof is a sensible choice.

Restoring to the original may not always be quite as simple as a straightforward conversion, for fireplaces usually suffer more at the hands of would-be improvers than any other part of a house. The small period cottage is no exception and many an original inglenook fireplace has been ruthlessly buried behind, first, a Victorian grate and, later, an 'all-night burner'.

Where there are back-to-back fireplaces and an axial chimney stack, the size of the chimney breast and the volume lost between the two rooms give a clue to the original structure. Excavation may reveal that it has been bricked up in two stages and at the final phase it reveals the simple brick-lined cavity that was built with the cottage, with – one hopes – the thick oak mantel-beam running across it. It is, of course, a major operation to excavate and restore a fireplace that may be up to 6ft across and 3ft deep, and it must be done under expert guidance, but the result is usually immensely rewarding and will give the cottage character as nothing else will.

After a fireplace is restored to the original, one is usually confronted with the problem of smoke control. In the old days people had enormous fires with plenty of draught to keep them going. Now we no longer want, or can afford, these huge fires, it is better to confine the fire to an inner fireplace and channel the draught by a hood tapering up into the flue.

If a closed solid-fuel unit is fitted, the simplest method is to have a fireclay liner put right up the chimney, thus preserving outward appearances. The use of modern heating appliances in an old chimney is apt to cause condensation, as the products of combustion of certain fuels, mainly sulphuric acid, cause progressive deterioration of the brickwork and stain the outer walls. This can only be cured by relining the flue.

Chimney stacks need careful inspection because of the danger of fire from faulty flues. The old stacks were built with wide bases to take

44 'Egg Cup' blends with a modern room-setting

huge fireplaces, and tapered like a pyramid as they reached the roof, but
when later generations added fireplaces and new flues they often cut
away part of the original structure without regard to safety. Provided
certain commonsense rules are followed the restoration of a fireplace
can be eminently satisfactory, and may, indeed, result in the structure
of the house being made safer than before.

But what of the future? With such a variety of materials now being
offered to the consumer it was felt that some drastic change was needed
to bring the fireplace into line with modern décor. The National Coal
Board therefore commissioned ocean-racing yacht designer Jon Bannenberg to design new fireplaces to answer the challenge of this space age
generation. His fifteen brand-new designs gave the English fireplace a
new image and revolutionised previous concepts of the traditional open
fire. Made in stainless steel, cast iron, brass, concrete, glass or burnished
wood, they appeal to the young trend-setting generation and blend in
very well with to-day's functional furniture and clean lines of architecture.

The Bannenberg fireplaces are brilliant and colourful, arresting enough to hold interest as pieces of sculpture in their own right, yet filling the basic need for a living open fire. The one shown on page 146 is aptly called Egg Cup, because of its shape. The sectional drawing (below) clearly shows its practicality. It is free-standing, made in cast iron and stove-enamelled in yellow or any other preferable colour. The suspended chain guard can be rotated to direct the heat wherever it is needed and it also acts as a spark guard. This is a fire that can be made to size or from basic prefabricated components and will merge in with modern décor in any room in the house (page 143).

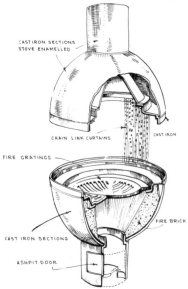

CAST IRON SECTIONS
STOVE ENAMELLED

CHAIN LINK CURTAINS

CAST IRON

FIRE GRATINGS

FIRE BRICK

CAST IRON SECTIONS

ASHPIT DOOR

45 Sectional drawing of Jon Bannenberg's 'Egg Cup'

Jon Bannenberg believes that fire has to be seen because it is not heard, and this is the basis of all his designs. In one he uses waves of stainless steel and red enamel to reflect the firelight right up to the ceiling; another is in a sculptured stepped style, which can be varied in the combination and type of material used for each step; another uses arches of stark vivid colour in simple formations. It is possible to fit cold cathode lighting between each colour and so emphasise the fire as a brilliant focal point (page 148).

46 Jon Bannenberg's 'Rainbow' design combines brilliant colour and lighting effects to emphasise the simple arch formations

An efficient-looking stove which has become very popular since its introduction is made of cast iron, stove-enamelled in a bright, cheerful red, designed to be free-standing or to go against a wall with the flue concealed.

There are, of course, some more orthodox designs for those who prefer them, but whether they are the conventional type or the more way-out, eye-catching arrangements, they all prove their point – that modern fireplace design can be linked to interior decoration with complete harmony.

All the Bannenberg designs are available, using the services of skilled builders, at varying prices. In some cases, designs can be reproduced using available building materials. In others, the components can be bought and incorporated into the construction. Detailed instructions for making these fireplaces are sold direct to the public and these include working drawings and details of materials, with names and addresses of suppliers and of qualified builders.

The do-it-yourself enthusiast has, in fact, a tremendous choice of materials and design. For instance, he can buy a fireplace kit of recon-structed stone, with a numbered stone-by-stone diagram to follow. Apart from the 4in thick rough-hewn stones to make the surround, the kit contains a stone hearth-slab, a stone or African mahogany mantel-shelf, shelves or flower-trough, according to the design selected. Mortar, cement, spirit-level, pointing trowel and anything else that may be needed are added!

For those who prefer tiles there is a kit that enables one to change the face of a fireplace in almost a matter of minutes. The panels that make up the hearth and surrounds are modular units of tiles which slide in and out when a change is required. The manufacturers provide a great number of possible combinations of designs from which to choose, so the fire face can be changed when a room is re-decorated or new furniture is brought in.

No great technical expertise is needed to design an individual fire-place surround. It is more a matter of commonsense and making sure that the materials chosen for use near the fire are incombustible. Some of the more obvious ones are polished marble, natural stone – polished,

47 Design from Spain, called 'Onion', in stainless steel. Its sleek lines look right in a modern room-setting

sawn or riven – brick, slate in various colours, ceramic fireplace tiles and metal tiles, smooth or textured.

There is no practical limit to the height of a fireplace, but there are other important dimensions to be noted, such as the overall width of the wall and the width and projection of the chimney breast, as well as the position of windows. Adequate hearth projection and/or a kerb is necessary because of the possible danger from falling embers.

The minimum distance for the use of combustible materials in front of an open fire or openable room heater is 12 inches and 9 inches in any other case. Six inches are required at the sides and back. The back distance generally depends on the thickness of the wall behind.

It is worth noting that the constructional hearth and the construction of the walling above the level of the hearth length should comply with the relevant Building Regulations. These can be bought from HM Stationery Office for approximately £1, or they can be consulted at a local library.

There are many firms specialising in supplying working drawings of fireplaces and replicas of classical patterns. The most recent move to date to dramatise the open fireplace has been made by the Solid Fuel Advisory Service (an alliance of the National Coal Board, the Chamber of Coal Traders, the National Carbonising Company, known as Rexco, Coalite and Chemical Products Ltd, and the Co-operative Fuel Trade Association). They asked five leading designers from France, Spain, Italy, Finland and Britain to submit ideas, and the result caused a minor sensation in the world of decorative art.

The Italian contribution by Lorenzo Papi and Bruno Sacchi, called Pyramid, is a foldaway fireplace in stainless steel, which can be supplied with contrasting metal sides. When not in use it looks like a piece of modern sculpture. From Finland's Timo Sarpaneva comes James, a vertical cylinder of stainless steel which includes a barbecue, a hot-plate cooking arrangement and an extension that takes a stereo, lighting and air-conditioning unit.

Jon Bannenberg, for Britain, designed Corona, a fireplace that can either be free-standing or recessed into the wall. It is a simple elliptical construction with four bars across the centre. Paco Munoz from Spain

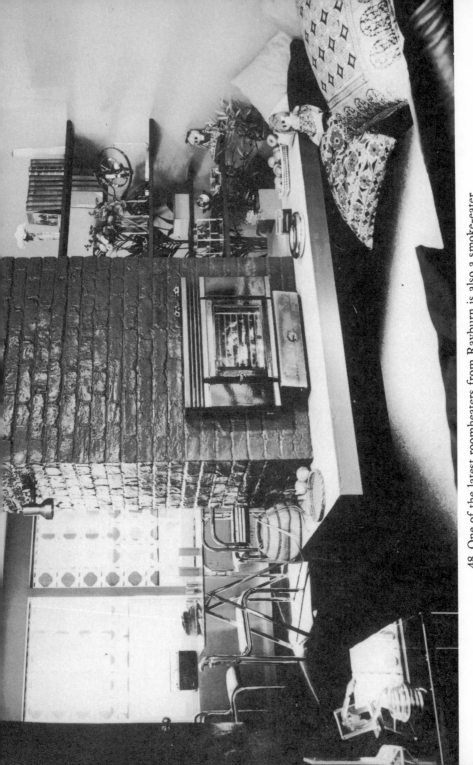

48 One of the latest roomheaters from Rayburn is also a smoke-eater

contributed a remarkable design called Onion, because it is precisely that shape. It is free-standing, gracefully moulded in stainless steel and the fire is seen through elliptical openings in the stainless steel skin (page 150).

There are several other advanced designs, some of which have provided sliding hoods that can be lowered to cover the fire when it is not in use. Most of these fireplaces are on sale from 'Living Fire Centres', or through selected installation companies. Prices vary, from about £100 upwards. Plans for some of the designs should also be available from the Solid Fuel Advisory Service.

However impressive the surrounds may look, the basic consideration must be the type of grate used and the performance of the flues if a fire is to achieve its purpose efficiently and economically.

We have come a long way from the old basket grate which just supported burning fuel with no means of control. True, we still have the old hole-in-the-wall, an Adam dog grate, a central fire and similar variations on old themes, designed to burn either coal or smokeless fuel, but they usually carry some form of adjustment to regulate the air supply to the fire and so control the rate of burning. Some have an underfloor draught, or a fan which revitalises a dying fire within a very short time.

It is possible to add a back boiler to many of these fires to provide hot water or central heating. If both are wanted, a high-output back boiler can be installed.

Convector fires set out into the fireplace have the advantage of giving out radiant heat as well as convected heat. The air continually flowing round the heated sides and back is warmed and returned to the room, and a throat restrictor is usually employed to minimise the amount of warm air escaping up the chimney. Free-standing convector fires give the same advantages.

What used to be known as a closed stove is now called a roomheater (shown, page 152), and many people prefer this to an open grate. It can be set into the fireplace or free-standing, with a glass front so that the flames can be seen, and burns with the efficiency and economy that a closed appliance offers. Roomheaters will also take boilers to supply partial or full central heating, thermostatically controlled, and can supply ducted warm-air heating. They all have 'shaking grates' which makes ash disposal easy.

Perhaps the most popular modern grate is the Baxi Burnall which offers the consumer no less than four different methods of ash disposal, all comparatively dust-free and with long intervals between each operation. This firm made a big breakthrough in solid-fuel heating in 1965. Providing a forced draught by means of a built-in fan was found to be particularly satisfactory with solid smokeless fuels.

Following the Smoke Control Act an appliance was recently designed that virtually consumed smoke before it went up the chimney, an electrically driven fan delivering air into a secondary combustion chamber where the soot and smoke are burnt away. The products that eventually go up the chimney are clean and smokeless. This 'smoke-eater' was developed by the National Coal Board in co-operation with the leading manufacturers. It has been a great success, enabling house-holders to burn certain types of low-grade coal even in areas which are smoke controlled.

Fuels

A vast amount of research has been going on into the production and packaging of coal products.

They can be divided into two broad classifications – the natural fuels, which can be bought sized and 'cleaned' to remove any impurities, and the processed, or manufactured fuels which are made from the natural ones.

The main types of processing are carbonisation and briquetting. Carbonisation makes the coal smokeless by baking it in large ovens and retorts to drive off the gases and tarry substances. These in turn are collected and used by the gas and chemical industries.

Briquetting is a similar process to that once employed for using up coal dust that could not be used in other ways. Nowadays, anthracite or Welsh dry steam coal produces very good ovoids and smokeless briquettes are made from bituminous coal.

The Solid Fuel Advisory Service gives free unbiased information, advice and technical assistance to members of the public and to the trades concerned on how to heat the home efficiently. An illustrated booklet, *A Housewife's Guide to Solid Fuel,* enables one to recognise the different solid fuels and to gauge their performance on different appliances.

Some coal merchants have a staff who are specially trained to give technical service, and these display a blue and yellow sign indicating their status. Others have signs which show that they are 'approved' or 'authorised' dealers, offering good service.

The National Fireplace Council has as its constituent members four major organisations, working together to provide a fully comprehensive service: the National Fireplace Manufacturers' Association, the Ceramic Fireplace Tile Council, the National Federation of Plumbers' and Builders' Merchants and the National Coal Board. Their main task is to ensure high standards of manufacture and to see that the best designs are available in showrooms all over the country for the public to see. For this purpose they have set up National Fireplace Centres in many cities and towns where the customer can be put in touch with specific manufacturers, and where advice is freely given on matters connected with fireplaces.

The sheer visual impact of modern designs for fireplaces have certainly helped the renaissance of the open fire. Other means of heating produce the required temperature but do not satisfy the artistic sense. We may also be more health-conscious, appreciating not only the continuous warmth but the fact that a flue helps to ventilate a house and keeps condensation to a minimum. Economics come into it, for the running costs of efficiently designed solid-fuel heating can be up to one-third less than with other fuels.

But most of all we are plainly and simply wanting the vital focal point that brings a room to life: 'log fires, lamplight and peace' are again making their appeal, for deep within us all is this urge to settle by the family fireside.

Appendix:

Fireplace Enquiries

The trade organisations listed below will put enquirers in touch with member firms who will supply information, advice and technical assistance where required.

The National Fireplace Council, Churchill House, Hanley, Stoke-on-Trent, Staffs.

The National Fireplace Manufacturers' Association, (at above address).

The Ceramic Fireplace Tile Council, Federation House, Station Road, Stoke-on-Trent, Staffs.

The National Federation of Plumbers' and Builders' Merchants, High Holborn House, 52–54, High Holborn, London WC1.

The National Coal Board, Hobart House, Grosvenor Place, London SW1.

The Scottish Tile, Fireplace and Domestic Heating Association, 22 Hanover Street, Edinburgh.

For Regional Lists of Approved Advice Centres

The Solid Fuel Advisory Service, Hobart House, Grosvenor Place, London SW1.

Index

157